THE JOURNEY TO THE
FATHER'S HEART

TIM SPYKSTRA

OCEANS
MINISTRIES

THE JOURNEY TO THE FATHER'S HEART

Published by Oceans Ministries
P.O. Box 461024
Aurora, CO 80046

ISBN 978-0-9862782-0-4

The Journey to the Father's Heart book and study journal may be purchased in bulk for educational, ministry, small groups, business, fund-raising, or sales promotional use. For information, please e-mail JourneyMaterials@oceansministries.org.

TABLE OF CONTENTS

INTRODUCTION

ACKNOWLEDGMENTS

I'm indebted to Michelle Wynia for her editing and valuable feedback as well as Bill Bierling and Danell Czarnecki.

A huge thanks to Henry Miersma and Central Creative Group for designing the cover and layout of the book and study journal. This project would not have happened without you.

A special thanks to Pastor Bryan Vander Tuig who encouraged me to write this book and took over my responsibilities at church as I wrote it. And to the all staff, elders, and the body of Christ at CrossPoint Church that released me in love to follow God's call on my life to share the message of this book outside the walls of the local church.

To my father Ray Spykstra who had the courage to admit his powerless and allow God's healing power to flow into our family.

My dear wife, Patty, who always makes me look good and has been my best friend and ministry partner for all these years. And to Sarah, TJ, and Anna, thanks for always loving and supporting your crazy dad, you have blessed me more than you will ever know.

Most importantly to my Abba, Father, it is all because of the life transforming love you have revealed to me that has made this book possible. May you receive all the glory!

INTRODUCTION

My two-year-old son was wrapped around my neck as we strolled through a bookstore. As I kept my son TJ confined from a potential disruption of the peace, my wife Patty was in another part of the store looking for children's books with my four-year-old daughter, Sarah. During our brisk hunt through the bookshelves, I had an encounter with God the Father that forever transformed my life. Right there in the middle of the store, I burst out in tears and laughter at the same time, something you would not have expected from someone as shy as I am.

The outburst was loud enough to cause my wife concern and she quickly made her way to the unsettling sounds to make sure everything was all right. Behind the stacks of tidy books and a neatly organized display of cards there I stood. I held my son firmly in one arm and a 5 x 7 picture in the other. I know my wife was relieved to find my surroundings intact, that I had not dropped TJ on his head or something worse in her brief absence.

Puzzled and concerned my wife and daughter approached; as they did so I lifted up the picture, tears streaming down my face. I felt as if the wind had been knocked out of me. I was speechless. For most people, walking by the picture section at a local bookstore may not have caused such an emotional upheaval; however, for me at that moment, that picture captured my soul like no other. Somehow the strokes of the artist's hand created an image that spoke to my heart. The young lad in the picture was not just any boy in any father's arms—it was me in my Father's arms.

Let me try to explain what I saw that monumental day. In the picture I observed a young boy around the age of two. He wore jean overalls and a white shirt. The boy's mouth was opened wide, depicting an unspeakable joy. On his head he wore a red football helmet dating back a generation. This energetic boy was hoisted high into the air by the strong hands of a Middle Eastern looking man with a beard and long wavy brown hair, dressed in white. The man's head was tilted back, eyes closed, and mouth slightly opened, showing his white teeth obviously displaying a father's delight in his son by his smile. This simple, but profound sketch spoke to me in an intimate way. It mirrored numerous unspoken childhood pains and tears, and at the same time created a new reality that initiated healing, unveiling a fresh path of freeing discovery, and hope for the future.

What I saw and heard in the depths of my being was, "Tim, you have always been my son; I have always been with you, even in the darkest times. And son, my heart loves you and rejoices over you; I will be your Daddy forever." For the first time in my life I knew without a doubt that I had a Dad who loved me completely, unconditionally, and eternally - a Dad who was proud of me in spite of failures, flaws, and frequent sins.

The reason this picture spoke to me in such a vivid, multi sensory way was because of my past. Although my past was filled with moments of hurt and disappointment, football was an advantageous outlet, and as far back as I can remember, I have always had a love for football. As a young boy growing up in Colorado, the Denver Bronco football games were what everyone lived for. Before the game everyone talked about who would win and after the game everyone would discuss the results. People talked about these things at church and the donut shop. So naturally cheering for my team sitting next to my dad was a big deal. Together we watched the games on the couch or on the floor and a few times I even got to attend a game live at the stadium. During those times I observed the various emotions my dad displayed during wins and losses and of course towards the referees. Spending time with my dad was important to me and even though his emotions swayed between exuberant elation to disappointment and annoyance at the game, I was still with my dad and desperately wanted his love and approval.

I will never forget the one Christmas I received my very own Denver Bronco uniform. At the age of five I already loved this game and was overjoyed when my uncle presented me with pants, shoulder pads and a helmet. My uncle who worked for the trash company at the time, found these treasures on the side of the road. The pants and shoulder pads were way too big, but my helmet fit and looked exactly like the one in the picture I described. I really did not care about any other gifts that year and anxiously put on the orange jersey, white pants and helmet and dashed out to my snowy backyard to play. I gave the neighbors hours of entertainment playing full football games, throwing, kicking, and running with the ball, always scoring the winning touchdown with opponents on my back without any real opponents or teammates besides my dog Muffy. It wasn't long before I convinced my parents to sign me up to play tackle football.

For the next 14 years, I played pee wee football, high school football and one year in college. Yes, I loved the game, but there was something deeper to it; football was a way to identify with my dad, a way to connect, to become someone of whom he would be proud. I clearly remember the times in high school when my dad would find me after the game on the field and hit me on my shoulder pads, and say, "Way to go, Tiger!" There was nothing like it.

However, that boy I described in the picture with the face lit up experiencing a heavenly joy, did not describe much of my childhood and early adult life. My dad battled alcoholism for as long as I could remember. As a teenager, my dad was introduced to alcohol, which helped numb the pain of his difficult family life. This battle with the bottle took its toll on my parents' marriage, and after many separations, my parents finally divorced when I was 10.

I have to admit that my love of the game of football was linked to the fact that while I was playing I was a world away from my problems. On the football field I was able to get out my anger and frustration in an acceptable way. Off the field I just wasn't sure what to do with these feelings of hurt and insecurity. Later on in my life I learned that this anger came because of fear - fear of an earthly father, fear of living in a shaky and unstable world, and even a deep fear of God the Father. This anger certainly helped my performance on the football field. I tackled my opponent on defense and on offense I attempted to dodge or run away from the other team. My anger however was not very beneficial at school, and I found myself in the principal's office on many occasions for fighting. In fact, I got to know the principal so well that I would eventually marry his daughter; God has a great sense of humor!

Thankfully, God's grace and love found me in the midst of a heart full of anger on a Sunday evening, November 26. As an insecure 13-year-old I walked forward to receive Christ's forgiveness and salvation on a cold Sunday night at a local church in Denver, Colorado. To this day, I can remember what I was wearing and where I was sitting in the sanctuary; that simple, yet powerful message by a visiting pastor from England, still rings in my ears. Through his words it became utterly clear to this boy filled with anger and hurt that Jesus had died for me, for all my sins and offered me a new life. Despite the fact that I had heard this truth many times before, I was overwhelmed by it at that particular moment. When an invitation was given to go to the altar and receive this gift of God's love, I was propelled out of my seat by an invisible force that brought me to the front of church. As I knelt before the altar, a man prayed these words over me, "Take this young man through the cross and hide him behind your cross forever."

When I lifted my head and opened my tear-filled eyes, my mother stood by my side. She too had tears streaming down her cheeks; tears of joy for God had heard her prayers and saved her son. How grateful I am for a godly mom that made church a priority, morning and evening, in spite of my many complaints and excuses. That night I did not sleep because I was overwhelmed by heaven's love. The next day at school, I spent most of the day overcome by what I had experienced. I knew I had been set on a new path; miraculously, the anger was being overshadowed and replaced with love and peace.

The Father was there for me; I just did not know it yet. He loved me through His Son Jesus, and comforted me with His Spirit, but the pain in my heart persisted. Since I was fearful of my earthly father, I was also fearful of my Heavenly Father. Since my earthly father was full of anger, I was sure I had done something to displease my Heavenly Father. The powerful and ever present picture of my earthly father still permeated my thoughts, and over time, distanced me from experiencing a complete relationship with God the Father. During my childhood and teenage years, I linked God to my alcoholic, angry and struggling dad. This was the father I was desperately trying to please and at the same time I feared him. In reality, this father-wound kept me from an authentic relationship with my earthly father and with God my heavenly Father. I ran from both of these fathers and greatly feared them.

Truly, I knew a loving Savior named Jesus, but God wanted me to encounter so much more of His heart. In the chapters that follow, a journey will unfold, a journey to the Father's heart, a journey that began that day when I held my son in one arm and a simple photo in the other. I am grateful to share that I now know and have experienced the healing of the Father's love. I have felt the full assurance of being His son! I proclaim the words from Romans 8:15, where the Apostle Paul states "For you did not receive a spirit that makes you a slave again to fear, but you received the Spirit of sonship. And by him we cry 'Abba Father [Daddy]".

CHAPTER 1

LOOKING FOR THE FATHER

I got my feet wet in ministry in an atypical way; instead of being called to a traditional church, I was asked by the president of the seminary from which I graduated to develop a prison ministry. While I was in school, I had the opportunity to preach the story of God's amazing grace up and down the state of California, in places like Folsom, San Quentin, Corcoran, and Donovan state prisons. It was a God-ordained time for me. A time to learn from prisoners about God's amazing grace and forgiveness, and the heart of Jesus that was so present in those prison chapels. Those men were so gracious to listen to a young punk from seminary who thought he had all the answers and the correct theology. In reality, God was speaking to me through the hearts of those broken men, and during those days, I got a tangible glimpse of the truth presented in the Gospel, in a way much different than the formal classroom setting.

God blessed those early years spent traveling up and down the California coast with whomever I could get to join me in this endeavor. The car rides with fellow brothers in Christ, and quality time spent behind prison walls with chaplains and inmates resulted in anointed appointments as the gospel fire spread up and down the state prison system. During this time I was also asked to plant a church with a professor from seminary, Dave Schuringa. Some of the first people that joined this new work called Wellspring were men recently released from the prisons. These men were invited into our homes for Bible study, we found jobs for them, some played on the praise team, and some were enrolled in seminary.

Yet, this newly formed group of church planters quickly found out that there were deep wounds and scars within these recently released believers. The struggles went way beyond the time spent locked behind bars. Yes, many knew Jesus Christ as their Savior and many even knew their

Bible better than some seminary students; however, the deeply embedded wound in their soul would drive them back into their former lifestyles. The unhealed, raw sore in their soul was more often than not linked to a father-wound. From my own experience, I would say that of all the men I have worked with in prison, at least 90 % of them had a poor relationship with their earthly father or never even knew their dad. The lack of a positive father-figure in the lives of these incarcerated adults is truly devastating not only to them but also to the children they father as the cycle continues.

Dr. David H. Schuringa, current President of Crossroad Bible Institute, an active, educating prison ministry for inmates worldwide, wrote an article entitled "The Most Meaningless Holiday of the Year." For those incarcerated, the most meaningless holiday is Father's Day. Schuringa shares, "Chaplains don't even bother handing out Father's Day cards like they do for Mother's Day." Many statistics from that article back up the blues for this holiday:

• Most inmates never had a parent read to them when they were children.

• Most inmates dropped out of high school.

• Most inmates were sexually and/or physically abused before age 12.

• Most inmates witnessed violence against others by the age 10.

• Most inmates were using drugs and/or alcohol by age 10.

• Most inmates suffered from severe neglect in "homes" that were in utter chaos 24/7.

• Indeed, most inmates grew up with no father in the home.

Dr. David H. Schuringa, "The Most Meaningless Holiday of the Year." i-newswire, 1 June 2005 http://www.i-newswire.com/the-most-meaningless-holiday-of/a22976

It is clear from this data that a majority of those convicted of a crime experienced unfortunate childhood situations. No caring parent would wish such a turbulent upbringing upon their child, and the outcome of such painful experiences often results in anger, violence and prison time. Deep wounds often manifested by the lack of a positive father-figure contribute to the obvious pandemic in the prison system in America that cannot keep up with the wounded hearts that break behind prison bars.

I have observed this wound in the hearts of prisoners, yet I have also seen this growing tsunami of pain in individuals who belong to churches; both groups experience often undefinable pain generated by father wounds. In our culture the divorce rate continues to climb to well over 50 percent; sadly, many dads have allowed themselves to be swept away from their homes. Many find themselves lured to pattern their lives after the deceptions with which they are inundated in the world in order to fill their own voids. Unfortunately, the cycle often continues and these children will grow up with a sense of insecurity that will imprison them for the rest of their lives unless healing occurs.

I could tell story after story of men, women and young adults who have come into my office plagued with overwhelming fear, addictions, poor self-image, a striving spirit, or bitter rage that consumes them, all because of the neglect of a father. One such woman, whom I will call Jane, grew up in a home where her dad was present physically, but that was it. He was a police officer, and definitely hardened by the effects of the job. When he returned home after work, he had nothing left for his family; he was emotionally and physically spent. Upon entering the home, he went straight to his alcohol to drink away his cares and ultimately his family. Jane continuously hoped for her dad's acceptance and approval. She wanted to be noticed and acknowledged. She longed for a hug, a smile, a compliment or some form of love coming her way. It never came, so she started looking for it elsewhere. Jane eventually became pregnant; she knew that if her father found out he would never forgive her. So she found a clinic and took the life of her baby all because she could not bear the shame of a father's scorn. Years later she came into my office a woman married with two kids, but still bleeding from the wounds of a disconnected father who still held her heart hostage.

Every one of us is Looking for the Love of a Father. Every human being desires an earthly father who loves, accepts and nurtures. Such a father or father-figure is vital for the healthy development of a child into a strong, mature adult. The presence of a father is fundamental to the family structure, for this is the way God created it. Earthly, God-fearing fathers are called to model the spiritual reality of the Father in Heaven. This perfect Father who created each individual desires that His children know His unconditional and perfect love. Not long ago I read an alarming quote that stated, "A child is not likely to find a Father in God unless He finds something of God in his father," (Austin, L. Sorensen). As a dad of three, this is both sobering and terrifying, yet I know in my heart that it is true; a dad is called to reflect the heart of the Heavenly Father.

Father. Dad. Daddy. Papa. I know I cherished the day when each of my children said the word, "Dadda." Much to my wife's dismay this was the name uttered first, despite the fact that she was the one who put in the most work! These are just a few of the names we call the male parent of a family. This paternal protector or provider is usually a term of endearment used by a toddler, teenager or an adult to define a specific person in their life. However, this was not the case for me. Just as anger permeated my childhood days, so fear walked hand–in-hand with the word father because of the environment in which I raised. As a result, my view of the heavenly Father was one of fear; he was someone from whom to keep a healthy distance. I had the hardest time dealing with God as Father; Jesus-yes, Holy Spirit-okay, but when it came to the Father; I did not want to go there. I would push that idea away; I would keep it in my head but not let it get too close to my heart. The idea of God the Father, the creator of the universe and all of mankind is something our human, finite minds cannot comprehend. God the Father is almighty and in control of all things and, because of sin, we want to be the ones who are strong and in charge. This deeper spiritual battle can be linked back to creation.

Adam and Eve, the crown of creation, were most alive in the presence of their Creator Father. Together they walked and talked with Him, they learned from Him, and above all, they knew perfect love from Him. The Garden was their serene home, their place of safety, of comfort, of unconditional love, and there they flourished. But the story takes a twist, a step backwards so to speak, as a false father comes; Jesus would call him the "father of lies" (John 8:44). The "serpent," Satan, told our first parents that they could live without the presence of God; they did not need a Father; they could do it on their own. Satan, disguised as a snake, assured Adam and Eve that if they ate from the tree of the "knowledge of good and evil," they would be "like God, knowing good and evil" (Genesis 3:5). He sold them on the notion of fatherlessness and he made it sound heavenly, but as they listened and followed, the result was much fear and anxiety. Adam and Eve tasted hell for the first time; the idea of life without the Father's covering entered their world, and as a result, their existence revealed for the first time their nakedness and shame.

The enemy's plan from the beginning was to falsify our understanding of the Father, to keep us from his presence and his perfect love. From the temptation of Adam and Eve to today, the "father of lies" has feverishly deceived believers and unbelievers into thinking that the Father is not necessary, and he has furthered this distorted plan by having one's imperfect earthly father linked to a Father who is ultimately a loving, gracious and forgiving Father. This is exactly what happened to me. But, the Good News is that the lies of the enemy cannot compete with the love of Abba Father. Our Daddy is on a mission, and that mission is to reveal His gigantic heart, a heart that will pour out rivers of His healing, restoring presence that will clothe nakedness and shame with garments of absolute belonging. He wants each of His children to know beyond doubt that each is his child. The One who spoke this world into being claims you as His and that makes you royalty.

You and I were created to belong; our DNA has encoded in it a need for another who is greater, who will always love and protect, whose very presence fills our soul with deep joy. This is clearly stated in the opening chapters of Genesis; it reads that God created us in His own image (Genesis 1:27). This means we look like our Dad; we look like the One who created us. The One who spoke the world into being is our Father, and the more we are in His presence, the more we grow into His likeness.

From the moment of our birth, each one of us has been on a journey to find the Father's love. Some have been misdirected by their earthly fathers; some have felt alone because of the nonexistence of a father. Even those who have fathers who have genuinely attempted to model a positive picture of our heavenly Father have fallen short and disappointed their children in some way. Our earthly fathers whether present or not are human and we learn from their shortcomings as ultimately we all need the unconditional love of Abba. This is the just the beginning, the beginning of a journey to experience a Father who is running to you. Jesus describes this so beautifully in the story of the lost son (Luke 15:11-32). In fact, the whole theme of the Bible can be summed up in the idea of the Father sprinting to you with arms open wide to embrace you; His face illuminated with total joy at the sight of you. He is inviting you to experience His love and grace and to offer you peace and contentment!

BEGIN YOUR JOURNEY:

Where are you at in your own personal journey to know the Father? The following questions, along with those provided at the end of subsequent chapters, are provided to help guide you along as you *Journey to the Father's Heart.*

Read the questions. Answer them honestly.

✤

1. In this chapter I site a quote that says "A child is not likely to find a Father in God unless He finds something of God in his father."

Does that statement ring true with you? Why or why not?

Has your earthly father helped or hindered your understand of God as a loving Father?

In Mark 14:36 Jesus is crying out to God in the depths of His pain and calls God "Abba", which means in Hebrew "Daddy" or "Papa". A word used by little Hebrew children showing complete trust in their fathers. Can you call God "Daddy" or "Papa," Why or why not?

2. Respond to my comment from the book that "from my own experience, I would say that of all the men I have worked with in prison, at least 90% of them had a poor relationship with their earthly father or never even knew their dad."

Do you think there is any correlation between crimes committed and the lack of a positive influence of a father in their lives?

Have you seen in others or experienced the painful effect yourself of not having a positive father figure in your life?

Do you think Satan has sought to diminish the role of the father in the family/culture in order to distort our view of God as a loving Father?

✣

3. Read Genesis 3 to see the enemy's plan and the effects of not living in a love relationship with the Father.

As you read verses 1-5 how does Satan attack the character of God as a trustworthy and loving Father?

List all the effects of living apart from the intimacy of the Father's love in verses 6 and following.

Can you identify with any of these effects in your own life (shame, fear, loneliness, etc.)?

In verses 8-9,14-15, and 21, the heart of the Father for His children is stated. How would you describe His affections for you in these passages?

Give examples from the New Testament where these affections are clearly seen.

JOURNEY DEEPER

Chose one of the four gospels (Matthew, Mark, Luke or John) and read it through in the next month. As you see Jesus in these texts make a note about His character, actions, and the words He speaks. Keep a list of what impresses you about Him and daily remind yourself that this is what my Father looks like (John 14:9).

PRAYER

Dear Father, as I start this journey to know your heart for me, I ask that you show me the truth of whom you really are. Lord break through any lies of the enemy that would distort your loving character and unleash the gift of your Holy Spirit to guide me on this life transforming journey. Even though I have tried to hide from you like Adam and Eve because of my sin and shame, I cry out for your presence. I lift my hands in surrender and ask you to take them and lead me to your heart. In Jesus' name, Amen!

❖

JOURNAL/NOTES

CHAPTER 2

UNDERSTANDING THE VALLEY

Ever since I turned sixteen and could drive I was able to help my dad out by driving a cement truck. Having a summer job waiting for me each year after college took the stress out of looking for a job, this was a way to earn money to help pay the cost of tuition, but was not easy work. I worked six very long days and was exhausted by Sunday. Yet, this summer was a bit different than before, as I was now married and graduated from college. I was ready to get on the job and save money for seminary in the fall. Already on my first day back, I noticed that my dad's drinking had worsened. The drinking was a daily occurrence that began routinely in the morning. I loved my dad, and it was heart-wrenching to watch this demon destroy his life. I knew I needed to confront him about his excessive drinking, but even the thought of bringing up the issue terrified me. Over the years both my older brother and sister had taken similar steps of "caring confrontation," which only resulted in strained relationships without any change in our dad's alcohol consumption.

My two older siblings and I all knew he needed help, and now the task of confrontation seemed to be on my shoulders. God had placed on my heart both an urgency and boldness to challenge my dad to please stop drinking. One early morning before the first cement delivery on a Saturday, I decided it would be the day. I told my dad that I loved him and that I could no longer allow alcohol to destroy his life. I nervously explained to him about a 40-day treatment center that our family had researched. I attempted to add that we were worried about him, wanted the best for him and that we were willing to come alongside him. We wanted our dad to be healthy and happy and agreed this next step would not be easy. I continued the one sided dialogue by boldly stating that I would give him a week to think about taking the steps to get help and concluded my conversation telling him that if he did not get help I would no longer be able to work for him.

My dad appeared shocked. He was speechless. I am sure these words came across as arrogant and ungrateful to his ears. After all, this was a great job with very good pay. Not waiting for a response, I hurried out of the office and jumped into the cement truck and drove off.

The rest of the week was business as usual. I arrived at 6 am ready to work and came home late tired and dirty and got up the next morning to start all over again. My dad never brought up anything about our conversation and neither did I. The next Saturday, exactly a week later, I arrived at work wondering how the day would end up. All day I kept contemplating what would happen. Finally, the last pour of the day was complete, and I was drove the cement truck back to the yard. With a pit in my stomach, I headed down the highway back to the yard; I rehearsed both scenarios in my head. Would I be relieved and saying, "Yeah, Dad, I am so proud of you! Together we can be done with this alcoholism!" Or would I be nervous and burdened, saying, "I am really sorry, Dad, but today will have to be my last day working for you."

As I pulled into the yard that late afternoon, there was no one left but my dad. I knew this would be the hardest thing I had ever done, but I felt I had no choice--this was life or death.

Upon my return, I was surprised to find a neatly folded note on the windshield of the truck that my Dad had let me drive to and from work. The note simply said, "Thanks for your concern, but I will take care of this on my own; I don't need anyone's help."

My heart dropped as I read those words. Confrontation had never been easy for me and now I was going to have to follow through on my word. Taking a deep breath I methodically entered the office and found my dad working at his desk. Somehow, someway words stumbled and stuttered out of my mouth and I let my dad know that as much as I needed the job, and as much as I wanted to help him, I could no longer watch him live this way. I could no longer work here and I could not be the one to make him stop drinking. The conversation did not go well; the words communicated by my dad were painful and spoken out of fear and anger, "Give me your keys!" he demanded. I cautiously handed him my keys to the company truck and left the office trembling, searching for the nearest pay phone. Just then the heavens broke forth in rain as if God wept along with me as I called my wife to pick me up in downtown Denver.

For the next few months I did not hear anything from my dad; the Father's Day card sent was returned unopened. It was a painful time, yet our family kept praying. Just as I had prayed every day for the past 15 years, my simple prayer was, "God, please heal my dad." But my prayer seemed even more hopeless as the days passed. Finally one night, I got a call from my step-mom. She said, "Your dad has entered a treatment center, Tim; I think he has hit his bottom."

As my dad would later share, he had come to the end of himself. He knew that it was either give up or get help; there was no other way out, nothing more he could do. He would learn during those 40 days of treatment that the first step to healing was to admit he was powerless over alcohol; that his life had become unmanageable. (Step 1 of Alcoholics Anonymous). Alcoholics Anonymous, or AA as it is commonly called, it is a 12-step program that, if truly embraced, will lead an individual to freedom from whatever addictive agent is keeping him in bondage. It is amazing to me that each of the 12 steps is based on biblical principles. As my dad courageously came to admit his powerlessness over alcohol, he took his first steps to freedom towards the Father's heart.

God would also use my dad's recovery experience to show me the way home, the way to the healing of Abba Father. Later when my dad came out to visit me during my first year of seminary, he found an AA meeting in the area and attended daily, and he invited me along. How different the meetings were from the seminary classes, chapels I attended, and even the church in which I worked. People smelled like smoke, the language was as colorful as the construction sites I worked on and there were people from all walks of life, from homeless people to corporate executives. I was overwhelmed by the bold honesty as each person would go around the room and introduce themselves saying, "Hi my name is Ray, and I'm an alcoholic." Most of those in the room knew they were powerless; understood the valley, the brokenness, and the need for a power greater than themselves.

I remember thinking to myself, "God, this is what you want your church to be like, this open, this honest. Our sin is too much for us to handle and we are stuck in a valley of darkness."

In the story of the lost son in Luke 15, transformation comes for the prodigal son after he spent his inheritance trying to fill the emptiness within his soul. Eventually, he ends up living and eating with the groveling pigs. When he comes to his senses, he recognizes he is in a dark place, one which he cannot get out of on his own (vs. 17). This is his first step toward the Father's heart. Each of us must come to this place, this place where we understand that we are not God, and the more we think we are as wise as God, often times the worse life becomes.

Our separation from the Father causes deep pain. Since the time of our first parents, Adam and Eve, we too have chosen to run away from the Father and to handle life on our own, which in the end only inflicts more pain. To fill the void of that pain, each and every one of us gravitates towards an addictive agent to heal the aching. A few examples would be:

Alcohol or drugs

Work, achievement, and success

Money addictions, such as overspending, gambling, hoarding

The need to control others; our kids, business, other relationships

Food addictions

Sexual addiction

Pleasing people (want everyone to like us)

Hero who is always rescuing others

Dependency on toxic relationships that continue to bring pain

Physical illness (hypochondria)

Working out, the rush of exercise

Adrenaline rushes, finding a riskier activity to find a new buzz

Cosmetics, clothes, cosmetic surgery, trying to look good on the outside

❖

Academic pursuits and excessive intellectualizing

Religiosity or religious legalism
(preoccupation with the form and the rules and regulations of religion, rather than benefiting from the real spiritual message)

Perfectionism

Cleaning, avoiding contamination, and other
obsessive-compulsive symptoms

Organizing, structuring (the need always to have everything in its place)

Materialism

Idolatry (giving one's heart and time to any created thing in order to ease your pain)

Can you find yourself anywhere on this list? Personally, I can find myself in not just one of these but many. The addiction or sinful cycle works like this: The pain is real, and ultimately can only be filled by the Father's love, but instead of reaching to Him for help, we reach for an addictive agent such as those listed above. At first the agent brings temporary relief but soon leads to negative consequences that bring about shame and guilt, which in the end result in additional pain or low self-esteem. So we jump right back into the chaos to find relief, and we spin deeper and deeper into the shadow of the valley of death.

Lynn had been attending our church for about a year when one Sunday after the morning service she approached me with loving humility and uttered these words that rocked my world. She said, "Pastor Tim, I really enjoy your preaching but..." Oh, how I hate those "buts." She quietly continued, "I sense you have a striving spirit." Somewhat in shock, I said, "What do you mean?" She went on to explain that she saw deep within my soul a spirit that kept pushing hard to achieve, to try to earn acceptance to receive love, ultimately the Father's love. She went on to say, "Pastor Tim, I'm praying for you and if at any time you want to join me in praying about this, I would love to meet with you." I politely thanked her, but what rushed through my mind was, "Who is this lady and why does she think she knows me so well? I don't need her prayers or help."

Does that language sound familiar? Yes, I was in denial, but those words haunted me, and through a number of circumstances that year, God continued to reveal a striving spirit that was alive and well in me, a spirit that was looking for love in all the wrong places. That spirit had been with me for a long time; it had become a friend, a way to deal with my wounds. It was with me as a five-year-old playing football striving to be seen, to earn love because of what I could achieve. It was with me when football ended after my first year of college, and when I started to feel tugged into the ministry and switched colleges. I switched from striving in sports to striving in academics. My goal was to be the top student, win the award for being the best Greek student in class, and to earn the respect of my professors.

After my education was finished my focus became ministry, to build a successful prison ministry, to build a growing vibrant church, to work as many hours as it would take at the expense of my wife and young family. This I could justify - it was for the LORD, for the cause of the Kingdom. Ultimately, I was striving to earn the Father's love, to somehow please Him, so that He would accept me, so that He would be proud of me. But no matter how hard I pushed, I never felt the pain go away; it still drove me to push harder, to do more. It was not enough, never enough.

I could identify with Paul's words in Romans 7 where he speaks of struggling to keep the law. Before He encountered Christ on the road to Damascus, he was by his own admission the best of the law keepers; he excelled in religion, and was the top dog in his class, so much so that it led him to hunt down Christians who were, in his mind, a huge threat to the true religion (Phil. 3:4-6). Paul had a striving spirit; he was addicted to religion. He was looking for the Father's love and thinking that he was finding it in his work, his religious system. Even after he came to Christ, that spirit was there as stated in Romans 7:14-25. In this passage of scripture, a spiritual wrestling match goes on within Paul, he desires to passionately live the law, he fervently wants to please God, but sin is ever present. In desperation he cries out, "...I see another law at work in the members of my body, waging war against the law of my mind and making me a prisoner of the law of sin at work within my members. What a wretched man I am! Who will rescue me from the body of death?"

Right there Paul opens up his heart to the journey home to His Father. He recognizes his dark place, the place he goes in his pain, his addictive agent for healing. He hopes that by living the law by being a good boy before God, he will find favor from the Father. However, all his good work, all his striving to keep the law falls short, he cannot do it, and the guilt is killing him. Indeed Paul understands the valley and admits he is powerless; he needs the pure love of God to come to His rescue. This is the place where God puts on His running shoes and starts sprinting to His children at blazing speed. Paul's confession leads to one of the most glorious passages of the entire Bible, Romans 8. In the next chapter, we will dive into the transformational words that God desires for every one of His children to hear.

But before we go there, glance once again at the list of the ways we handle pain. As you read through the list, ask God to speak to you. Can you find yourself identifying with any of the points? Are there things you are doing at this moment to manage your pain, your wounded heart? To be honest, as I look at the list I can see myself running to some of those things again to deal with new challenges in my life. I need to continually cry out, "Hi, my name is Tim; I am powerless over my sin!" Will you join me in this declaration: "Hi, my name is _____; I am powerless over my sin!"

CONTINUE YOUR JOURNEY:

1. In this chapter I mentioned that my father's journey to healing came by way of encountering the 12 steps of Alcoholics Anonymous. Step 1 states that "we are powerless over alcohol; that life has become unmanageable."

We struggle to understand the word "powerless" in our culture, what do you think that word means?

Read Luke 15:11-20. *When did the "lost son" come to understand that he was "powerless," or as they say in AA "hit the bottom?"*

In verse 17 we read that the "lost son" had "come to his senses" and he re-alized that he could no longer live apart from the father. He had tried and it landed him face down in pig poop. To come to our "senses" is truly a gift from God, to hit bottom and realize we can't do life anymore on our own is a gift. Before you move on take some time and ask God to shine His light on your heart and reveal anything that is keeping you from knowing the Father's love.

A list of 20 addictive agents is mentioned in this chapter. As you re-read the list what ones do you gravitate to in order to escape the pain? Feel free to add your own to the list. Be honest here; as it is the first step to experi-encing the journey to the Father's heart and begin the steps of experienc-ing true love and acceptance.

2. As I shared with you my battle was a "striving spirit" or it could also be described as a "religious spirit." I felt if I was good enough and worked hard enough God the Father would love me. This was insanity because I kept feeling that I was falling short and continually needed to do more and be more. Take some time right now and read Romans 7:7-35, soak in Paul's words as he battles a religious spirit.

How did Paul try to find acceptance and love from the Father?

Have you ever experienced the same battle waging in your mind as you deal with your sinful nature?

Describe where this "religious spirit" landed Paul as read in verse 24? Have you ever been at the same point in your life?

Paul's pit of powerlessness led him to look up for outside help. Who does He see according to verse 25?

JOURNEY DEEPER

To be honest about your powerless or your spiritual pit is key to the journey to the Father's heart. Make a list of sinful habits or addictions that you run to instead of the Father's love. As you prayerfully come up with your list find someone that you trust to share the list with. You may want to consider a 12-step program or a support group in your local church to help you live honestly.

PRAYER

Abba Father, I ask you to help me come to my senses and understand the valley that I am in. Please reveal to me the places and times in my life when I run away from your presence through addictions and sin with the temporary benefit of numbing the pain that only you can heal. Father it is so hard to be honest with myself and others, please grant me the courage to overcome my fear of what others think and trust that your love and acceptance is all that I need. Lord bring me to the place where I can honestly say "Hi, my name is _____ and I am powerless over my sin!" Amen!

JOURNAL/NOTES

✤

CHAPTER 3

THE FATHER'S LOVE DISPLAYED

The other night my daughter rushed into the house after her church youth group and said, "Dad! You've got to watch what we saw tonight; it will make you cry." She pulled up the clip for me, and together we sat, eyes glued to the screen. She was right, tears were my only response. The clip came from a short, award-winning foreign movie called "Most" (in English "The Bridge"). Let me try to capture a bit of the story.

There is a man who has a son, whom he raised on his own, and whom he loves very much. The man works as a bridge master for the railroad. The son loves watching the trains and the people who travel on them. As this young son watches the people traveling on the trains he seems to see into the depths of the travelers' hearts and know who they really were. There are people who were lonely, angry, selfish, hurting and addicted. One day, the father takes the son to work with him; as the dad does his job of raising and lowering the bridge, the young boy spends his time fishing in the river below. The dad keeps a watchful eye on the son and is delighted by the joy he has fishing.

In the midst of this perfect father-and-son day, a tragic mistake happens. An approaching train fails to notice the red light on the track that warns that the bridge is up for boats to pass under. As the father watches the boat safely passing below, the son hears the whistle of the train and sees the impending danger. The father had shown his son how to pull the lever that would lower the bridge, and so the boy runs up the bank of the river and opens the hatch to get to the lever. As the father looks to the river where he anticipates seeing his son, he notices the fishing pole but does not see his son. Just then, the father catches sight of two awful realities; first, the train approaching the raised bridge and second, his only son slipping into the hatch beneath the iron support that lowers the bridge. He realizes that if the bridge is lowered his son will be crushed, but if the bridge is not lowered, the train full of passengers will be doomed.

The father faces a horrific choice, lower the bridge and save the lonely, selfish, hurting people on the train or leave the bridge up and save his beloved son. In utter agony, the father grabs the metal lever and thrusts downward, crushing his son below. He runs out of his control booth as the train passes by; with overwhelming anguish torturing his soul, he cries out, looking into the windows of the train at the people who are clueless that their lives have been spared by a father who loved his son more than life. Words cannot describe the sacrifice he made. It was truly an incredible display of love beyond measure.

However, on the train, there is one young lady in the bathroom preparing to shoot drugs into her veins; for some reason, she looks up and glances out the window of the train and her eyes perceive the face of the man, and at the sight of his inexpressible anguish, she drops the needle to the floor. That one glance from the father forever changes the course of that young lady's life; she encounters a change of direction, a link to hope outside of her addictive agent to heal the hurt. The next scene of the movie shows the father grieving the death of his son as he picks up his crushed body and carries his son down the same tracks he had once walked hand-in-hand with his son.

The story line concludes with a scene a few years later. Both the father and the young lady from the train window walk along the same busy street. Something about this young lady catches the father's attention and he recognizes her as a passenger of the train on that dreadful day a few years back; this woman's face is full of smiles as she tightly hugs her own boy in her arms. As she walks past the father, he notices her joy and the joy in the face of her son; and the father begins to smile. At that moment, he that realizes the sacrifice of his son brought life; his son's death was not in vain. The movie ends with the father throwing his arms up in the air, celebrating the victory of the sacrifice.

After watching the video, I wiped my tears and sat in silence. Through this story, John 3:16 came to life; "God so loved the world that He gave His only Son, that whoever believes in Him shall not perish but have eternal life." So often for me, the focus of this verse has been on the work of Jesus on the cross; it should be--that is important. Yet, I have failed to comprehend that the Father is the one who gave up his Son, his Son with whom he walked before time, this Son whom he loved perfectly, and who loved Him perfectly. It was God's love for this fallen world, for sinners like you and me, which caused him to pull the lever and crush his only Son. What did the Father's face look like as Jesus was crushed on the cross for the sins of people who lived rebellious lives, for people who had no clue of the sacrifice that was taking place? Oh, the anguish in the Father's heart as he gave up his Son for us, the ones on the train traveling by oblivious to the cost of the sacrifice for salvation.

Picture the pain and sacrifice the Father went through; imagine the pain on His face; imagine what that looked like as you passed by on your train. God the Father sent his Son and let him die in your place so that you can be reunited with your Father, so that you can really live, so that the addictions, the anger, the loneliness of a life lived without the Father can forever be taken away. Like the young lady, your sins can be dropped on the floor like her heroine needle; you can leave behind that addictive agent, whatever it is. The Father's face turns towards you; the Father's love reaches out through the death and resurrection of his Son. He alone can give you the life for which you were made, a life of "joy unspeakable and full of glory" (1 Peter 1:8).

Many times we stop our reading at John 3:16 and we miss the blessings that follow from the Father. Verses 17-18 state, "For God did not send his Son into the world to condemn the world but to save the world through Him. Whoever believes in him is not condemned, but whoever does not believe stands condemned already because he has not believed in the name of God's one and only Son." This is the heart of the Father's love, pure love; that is the best way to describe God; He shows His love in Jesus, his life and his death. He desires for you to receive this powerful love; this love which words cannot yet describe this love that frees believers from any condemnation and erases any wrongdoing in God's eyes.

Remember where we left off in our last chapter? Paul cried out in his powerlessness, "What a wretched man I am! Who will rescue me from this body of death" (Romans 7:24)? In other words, who's going to save me from the train of destruction on which I ride? The answer is given in verse 25, "Thanks be to God – through Jesus Christ our Lord!" Paul, in the midst of his valley of brokenness, cries out for help and is reminded by the Spirit that God the Father loves Him and has rescued him through his only Son, Jesus. Paul is directed back to the gift of the Father's love and the Father's love is fully displayed in the Son.

Over time, God has continued to heal my heart, and much of that healing has come from reading the first four books of the New Testament. The life of Jesus, the miracles of Jesus and the teachings of Jesus in these gospels overtly display the Father's heart. In the book of John, a conversation occurs between Jesus and one of his disciples, prompting Jesus to say, "I am the way, the truth, and the life. No one comes to the Father except through me. If you really knew me, you would know my Father as well. From now on, you do know him and have seen him" (John 14:6-7). The disciple responds to this and says, "Lord, show us the Father and that will be enough for us" (vs. 8). This statement is a profound truth spoken from the mouth of one of the twelve disciples. If only each of us would somehow realize that knowing the Father is enough. One glimpse of the Father's face and the Father's love brings about transformation. In the story of the lost son, Jesus is the running Father (Luke 15). He is running to you and to me in our brokenness!

The follower of Jesus who is involved in this dialogue is Philip. Philip, the disciple from Galilee, the one who beckoned Nathaniel to join him in following this rabbi, Jesus; this is the disciple to which Jesus responds with love and conviction. "Don't you know me, Philip, even after I have been among you such a long time? Anyone who has seen me has seen the Father. How can you say, 'Show us the Father?' Don't you believe that I am in the Father, and that the Father is in me? The words I say to you are not just my own. Rather, it is the Father living in me, who is doing his work" (John 14:9-10). Even after following Jesus practically everywhere he went, his disciples have difficulty understanding this concept. So Jesus takes this opportune moment, knowing that his time is short, to show not only his disciples of ancient days but also us that he is mystically tied to the Father. John 14 powerfully establishes the relationship between God the Father and God the Son. If you take time to read this scripture on your own, you will count 23 times that Jesus uses "Father." Other passages that strongly link the Father and Son together are found in John 13-17. In this final teaching time before the cross, the Father's name is mentioned 48 times.

This is a crucial point that cannot be missed. This is where the Father displayed his ultimate love for us. God sent his Son Jesus on a mission not only to die on the cross, be resurrected from the dead and be seated at the right hand of God, but also to show us his love. He desires for us to trust him, and through faith believe in him. On our own we can never earn the Father's love, forgiveness or acceptance. We cannot be good enough, intelligent enough, athletic enough, rich enough, beautiful enough, musical enough, popular enough, successful enough, you name it. But, through the sacrifice of Jesus and by believing on his name we can boldly declare with the apostle Paul our privileged position:

Therefore, there is now no condemnation [or nothing that keeps us from the Father's love] for those who are in Christ Jesus, because through Christ Jesus, the law of the Spirit of life set me free from the law of sin and death...... And so he condemned sin in sinful man, in order that the righteous requirements of the law might be fully met in us, who do not live according to the sinful nature but according to the Spirit... (Roman 8:1-4)

Did you comprehend this? You are covered by Jesus' perfect blood. You are accepted by the Father. When Jesus died and was put into the tomb, and the rock was rolled over the mouth of it, your backpack was full of sin, yet because Jesus was the atoning lamb our sins are forever buried! These sins are never to be held against you by the Father. And when Christ was raised from the dead, you were joined to him in a new life of freedom, empowered by the very presence of Jesus living in you through the Holy Spirit. You live as Jesus does with the glorious love and acceptance of the Father.

The death and resurrection of Jesus is the key to seeing the Father's love displayed. The cross upon which Christ suffered and died preaches to us in such profound ways! This story of a well-loved priest and his simple sermon illustrate the inexplicable power of the cross.

A priest from a small village announced to his congregation that he was going to preach his last and greatest sermon the following Sunday. Word quickly spread through the town and the church was packed. Many wanted to witness the last and greatest message of the elderly priest. As the priest opened the doors and walked reverently into the sanctuary, the crowd hushed preparing for the much anticipated words of the priest. As he walked to the front of the altar, he gently removed a burning candle from the stand and proceeded to walk to a large crucifix hanging in the front of the sanctuary. Lifting his shaky and aged hand, he held the candle first to the nailed feet of Jesus; after a moment, he raised the candle to the pierced side of the Savior and paused for a time. Next, he positioned a stepping stool so that he could climb up to the scarred hands of the wounded healer, and allowed the congregation to see the outstretched hands in the candle-light. He climbed up one step higher on the stool and brought all eyes in the room to see the face of the bloodied King. He elevated the candle for as long as he could to highlight the face of the beloved Lord, and when his strength failed, he climbed down, returned the candle to its proper place and quietly sauntered out of the building without saying a word. The congregation was speechless. Truly this was to be a sermon forever seared in their hearts and minds.

Indeed, let the cross speak to you wherever you are today, absorb the truth that Christ's suffering was not in vain but for your redemption and my redemption. Accept the gift of salvation and come alongside those sitting in the pew that day watching the elderly priest and gaze at the gift of the Father running to you in the Son. See the face of the Father in the face of Jesus, see the pain and the heartache experienced all for you, all so that you can walk into the arms of a waiting Father where you are totally and forever forgiven. There you are not condemned, shamed, or judged, but you will receive a love that liberates and a life of belonging that words cannot express.

CONTINUE YOUR JOURNEY:

1. Take a moment to watch the short story described at the beginning of this chapter: http://www.oceansministries.org/the-bridge/.

If you were the father in this story what do you think you would have done?

Why is this short story so powerful?

Take a few minutes and meditate on John 3:16-18. What motivated the Father's gift of His "only son?"

According to verses 17-18, what is the heart of the Father's powerful love in Jesus for you? Look at this same theme found in Romans 7:24-8:1-4.

What do you think it means to live a life with "no condemnation" from your Heavenly Father?"

2. In this chapter I make the statement that "...God has continued to heal my heart, and much of that healing has come from reading the first four books of the New Testament. The life of Jesus, the miracles of Jesus and the teachings of Jesus in these gospels overtly display the Father's heart."

When you look at Jesus describe who you see?

According to John 14:6-14 what is Jesus' main mission?

Philip says to Jesus, "show us the Father and that will be enough for us," (vs. 8). How would coming to know the Father through Jesus be "enough" for you? How would you live differently?

Jesus makes a crazy bold statement in vs. 12, "I tell you the truth, anyone who has faith in me will do what I have been doing. He will do even greater things than these, because I am going to the Father." Do you believe that if we come to know Jesus as the one who leads us to the heart of the Father, we can live with the same power and authority as Jesus did as sons and daughters of the Father? Again, how would you live differently?

JOURNEY DEEPER

Read one of the accounts of Jesus' death or find a cross or picture of one, and just "be still" for a few moments. Let the Spirit of the Father reveal His love and receive it. Say to yourself: "This was done for me!" Jesus declares, "I tell the truth, whoever hears my word and believes him who sent me has eternal life and will not be condemned; he has crossed over from death to life" (John 5:24). Claim this promise!

PRAYER

Dear Father God, I confess today that I need you and your powerful love shown through the death of your Son Jesus Christ. I know that my sin caused me to run from the love that I need the most. Please forgive me of my wandering heart. Today I receive the gift of your only Son who took my place on the cross to pay completely for all my sin. I also believe that as Jesus was raised from the dead so too I have been given new life as a child of God. I thank you for this amazing gift of love that is forever mine, Father you have my heart now and forever, Amen!

JOURNAL/NOTES

CHAPTER 4

OUR GUIDE AND THE FAITHFUL FATHER

In J.R R. Tolkien's well-known book and movie *The Hobbit,* there is a wise wizard named Gandalf who tells a reluctant and unlikely hero, Bilbo Baggins, "There is more to you than you know." At the time Bilbo was living in a lush, hilly countryside called The Shire. He is perfectly content to live the remainder of his days by himself in this peaceful village, safe and secure in his tidy hobbit hole. Yet, Gandalf's words awaken something within this somewhat self-absorbed Bilbo Baggins. An excursion awaits Bilbo, one that will be full of things unknown and allow him to discover that he has been created for more than the selfish and sedentary life he is currently living.

We have a wise messenger, like Gandalf, that is reminding each of us, "There is more to you than you know." There is royalty surging through your veins, you belong to Me, you have been made for more than you know; you have a story to tell! Oh yes, there is an enemy who attempts to hold you in a hole and who desires to convince you that what you have right now is all you need in life. Play it safe, take care of only yourself, and do not embark outside of your comfortable hobbit hole. The enemy has sought to cloud your view of the Father, knowing that if you understand your true identity, the lies will lose all power over your life.

When Gandalf comes into Bilbo's homey hole, he brings with him a dozen motley dwarfs who turn the neat dwelling into a den of chaos as these un-familiar guests devour every last drop of wine and every morsel of Bilbo's food. After the fellowshipping settles down, the dwarves plop down by the fireplace and begin to sing an ancient song. As Bilbo listens, "some-thing Tookish woke up inside of him, and he wished to go and see the great mountains, and hear the pine-trees and the waterfalls, and explore the caves, and wear a sword instead of a walking stick" *(Shmoop Editorial Team, "Wealth Quotes: The Hobbit, or, There and Back Again," Shmoop University, Inc., 11 November 2008, http://www.shmoop.com/hobbit/wealth-quotes.html).* Our loving Father wants us to know our true identity. He wants us to experience more than surface friendships and collect earthly stuff, He desires us to find true unconditional love and sustenance in the place of perfect peace with the Father. He does not want us to be locked in fear, selfishness and complacency, afraid to become all that we were intended to be.

The guide who awakens Bilbo to see beyond himself is Gandalf; and the Guide who awakens us and leads us on the journey is the Holy Spirit. He is the gift of the Father; he opens our eyes to see the Father and our true identity in His perfect love. In Romans 8, this Guide is mentioned 18 times; truly the apostle Paul wants his reader to know that the Spirit's work is profound and powerful. Bilbo would have never survived his everyday life or epic adventures without Gandalf the magician. So, too, we would be overwhelmed and weighed down by our unworthiness and self-regard without the Spirit's presence.

In Romans 8:2, Paul calls the Holy Spirit "the Spirit of life who set me free from the law of sin and death." The writer teaches that it is the Spirit who brings one to Jesus. We would have remained in a state of spiritual death, separated from the Father's love, forever in our own hobbit hole, unless the Spirit opened the door of our heart and revealed to us the saving work of Jesus Christ. Our Guide constantly points us to Jesus and His saving work. He does not want us to forget the greatest historic event in history, the day that the Father gave the Son to die in our place so that none of our sins would be held against us. This sacrificial act allows our relationship to be fully restored to the Father.

My favorite Sunday of the month at my local church is when we celebrate communion. As a church family, we gather to eat and drink spiritually from the cross of Jesus. During this sacrament, the Holy Spirit always seems to show up and remind me, "Tim, taste and see my love for you, my blood and broken body is enough for you; you belong to me forever." I leave those intimate times of communion with a deep sense that I'm part of this mysterious heavenly family. I am reminded of God's great grace, the gift of forgiveness given to me; I have been forever washed in the blood of the Lamb. Oh, what a marvelous work of the Spirit living in me.

The Holy Spirit, our Guide, not only reminds us of the cross, but also changes the way we think and act so that over time we may develop more and more of the mind of Christ. The Spirit is leading us on this journey to learn to think like Jesus did as he walked this earth. If you recall, Jesus' whole mission was wrapped up in His love for the Father and knowing His Father's love for Him. The Apostle Paul says in Romans 8:5-6, *"Those who live according to the nature have their minds set on what the nature desires; but those who live in accordance with the Spirit have their minds set on what the Spirit desires. The mind of sinful man is death but the mind controlled by the Spirit is life and peace."*

With the help of the Spirit we can live a life of peace and hope. We do not need to be rooted in the woes of the world and stay within in our safe homes and churches for security. We can set our minds on the things of Christ, we can be overcomers! But what does this love relationship look like that Jesus modeled for us? Jesus explains it to us when he answers this question, "Teacher, which is the greatest commandment in the Law?" Jesus responds: "love the Lord your God with all your heart and with all your soul and with all your mind.' This is the first and greatest commandment. And the second is like it: 'Love your neighbor as yourself.' All the Law and the Prophets hang on these two commandments." (Matthew 22:37-40)

Jesus loved his Father and demonstrated it by trusting His will no matter how dark and uncertain things may have seemed. This is evident in the Garden of Gethsemane when Jesus calls out, "Abba Father, everything is possible for you. Take this cup from me. Yet not what I will, but what you will" (Mark 14:36). Dying and bearing the burden of sin was not a task to be taken lightly. With this act of obedience came extreme physical and emotional pain, and yet, Jesus submitted to the will of his Father. Thus, Jesus deeply loved the Lord with all his heart, soul and mind. What an authentic and trusting relationship with his heavenly Father.

Jesus also demonstrated genuine love for his neighbors, even in the midst of pain and turmoil on the cross. Through the power of the Holy Spirit, Jesus was able to speak the following words: "Father forgive them, for they do not know what they are doing" (Luke 23:34). His words leave me speechless. Jesus is talking about the ones who plotted and planned his death, the ones who drove the nails in his wrists and feet, the ones who spat upon him and mocked him. If you and I are going to be led by the Holy Spirit on this journey and live in a love relationship with the Father as Jesus did, we will need to be led in love. We will need to trust the Holy Spirit's leading as well.

The Holy Spirit's work is to bring us to and keep us in Abba's love forever. As Paul says in Romans 8:12-14, "Therefore brothers we have an obligation – but it is not to the sinful nature, to live according to it. For if you live according to the sinful nature you will die; but if by the Spirit you put to death the misdeeds of the body, you will live, because those who are led by the Spirit of God are sons [daughters] of God."

For us to understand more and more of Abba's love, we need to have faith in the Father and learn to live the way of the cross, which is the way of forgiveness, just as Jesus did. These two actions of love have done more for me than anything else as I slowly became more and more aware of Abba's presence in my life.

What a faithful Father we have! If only we can truly see this. Time after time Jesus points us to that Father. On a recent visit back to Colorado, I was once again made aware of this faithful Father. While sharing a meal with my dad, brother, sister and their families, a vivid and meaningful conversation took place. After dinner, my dad felt led to share with all of us some of his thoughts at the time of our parent's divorce. He told us how he realized that he had not been the father he should have been and had often prayed this prayer: "God, I have not been a very good father to my three kids and now they will be without a father in the home; I give them over to you. Will you show yourself to be a faithful Father to them?" My dad's sincere words blessed all of us and God truly heard my earthly father's prayer. Over the years all three of us kids could point to many times that the Father's faithfulness was made evident in our lives.

One such tangible way occurred when my brother, sister, and I were still in school. Food was sparse, and a bag of groceries showed up at our doorstep. Another time, our heavenly Father orchestrated a large check to be sent in the mail to help pay a Christian school bill my mom could not afford. This faithful Father was seen in wonderful grandparents who offered a haven of rest in the midst of a storm. He worked through a loving grandfather who taught my brother Curt and me how to work the good old-fashioned way by helping us start and run our own lawn mowing service.

The father was present at high school football games when, after fumbling the football and running off the field in self-disgust, I was told to get back on the field and not allowed to quit. The Father's love showed through my coaches that they still believed in me no matter how bad the mistake. He showed up on my wedding day by walking my high school sweetheart down the aisle and into my heart, and all the while providing for me years of sacrificial love and support.

The Father showed up during my seminary education with funds from unknown sources to help pay bills that my wife and I could not have paid on our own. He showed up at the birth of my children, at the death of loved ones. In the deepest darkest valleys of ministry seasons and at the mountaintops of elation, he was present. Even in the midst of writing these words, my legs get weak, a sign that Abba is in the room looking over my shoulder and shining on me with ever-present eyes of love.

When I pause and look back on my life there is overwhelming evidence of the Father's huge hands providing and directing every single step of my life and those of my family members. He was in the midst of every trial and struggle holding each of us up and bringing us through. And as my sister Cindy loves to say, "He turned the horrific volcanic eruptions into beautiful islands that display His glory." His everlasting love was evident!

I have learned over the years that the more I cry out to Him when I am overwhelmed or cannot understand, and simply say the words, "Abba, not my will but your will be done," somehow I experience peace. Or, in the words of a dear sister in Christ who has gone through countless surgeries and disappointments boldly say, "God, you've got this." Speaking those

⚜

words of release and submission help me refocus and remind me of the truth. And the truth is--He has always been there! Again and again I have to be reminded of this! I lose sight of my faithful Father when I try to obtain what the world says is important or to control where I think life should go. In other words when I feel I have to "be God" I actually push him away. When I become so wrapped up in me, I lose awareness of His presence. Yet, when I take the time to bask in the Father and his love for me, I remember that I have a Counselor and Guide who is right by my side, even when I am not aware of his presence. The Holy Spirit is constantly guiding each one of us, prompting us to let go and let God.

Learning to trust God the Father's faithfulness has been an ongoing, life-long journey for me. I clearly remember a day when God had to shake me up to wake me up. It was in the midst of a church league basketball game. I was lying on the gym floor, I had seriously wrenched my ankle, and in anger, began to pound the floor and cry. These strong and rather inappropriate behaviors were not due to the pain I was experiencing from the chipped bone in my ankle, but because of the anguish in my heart. I was mad at God because things were not turning out the way I thought they should. I was putting a tremendous amount of time and effort into his church, I was striving to build a successful ministry, to become a great pastor to all of the sheep, and be the perfect husband and father, and in my gut, things seemed to be falling apart. I was utterly exhausted. I felt like a failure and right there on the court, I wondered where in the world God was in all of this.

You are more than you know! You have been created to live wrapped in the Father's arms of love. May you trust the Holy Spirit as He guides you on this journey. Learn to leave your hobbit hole and venture out in faith, trusting in your faithful Father. Give him your will, let your will die with Jesus on the cross, and let the Holy Spirit resurrect you into the life of Jesus, where you seek to love the Father with your whole life.

Little did I know God was right there at center court with me waiting for me to trust Him and say "Abba, not my will but your will in my life; here you go, please take it." This season of brokenness became a gift from God.

During this time he clearly showed me my striving spirit and my need to seek forgiveness and return to trusting in His faithfulness. Deuteronomy 6:5 says to "love the Lord your God with all my heart, soul, mind, and strength," this was a scripture that ministered to me. However this was not enough, the Holy Spirit wasn't through with me during this season, I not only needed to learn to love him with all my being but also be able to love my neighbor as myself as stated in Matthew 22:39.

What does that mean to love your neighbor as yourself? The next chapter on forgiveness will address that very important topic. If I cannot love myself for who God created me to be, how can I love anyone else?

CONTINUE YOUR JOURNEY:

1. What is your reaction to the statement, "There is more to you than you know. There is royalty surging through your veins, you belong to Me, you have been made for more than you know, you have a story to tell."

Do you ever feel a nudge in your soul that God is calling you out of a comfortable place to something epic beyond what your mind can conceive?

What holds you back from following that nudge or calling?

2. Take some time and read through one of the most powerful chapters in the bible, Romans 8.

Our Guide on this epic journey is mentioned 18 times in this chapter. Who is He?

As you read verses 1-4, to whom does the Holy Spirit constantly direct us to on this journey to the Father's heart?

The Spirit not only points us to Jesus and his powerful work on the cross but as you read Romans 8:5-6 you will note that he will help you change what?

As the Spirit changes our thinking and gives us more of the mind of Christ we will be filled with the power to love like Jesus did. According to Jesus what are the two greatest loves that He calls us to Matthew 22:37-40?

Give examples from the Gospels where you see the Holy Spirit giving Jesus power to love His Father as well as the neighbors around him. This would also include his enemies.

Once again read Romans 8:12-14. Notice that if you choose not to live like Jesus and in the love and power of the Spirit, there is a death that takes place in our heart and limits us from really living. Yet, if we allow the Spirit to lead us we will experience the indescribable security of being children of God. Share a time in your life when you felt spiritually dead. What do you think was the cause?

Describe a time when you felt spiritually alive? How did you see the faith-ful hand of your Father directing you?

JOURNEY DEEPER

Go back to the greatest commandment in the bible given by Jesus, "to love the Lord you God with all your heart and with all your soul and with all your mind.' This is the first and greatest commandment. And the second is like it: 'Love your neighbor as yourself.' All the Law and the Prophets hang on these two commandments," (Matthew 22:37-40). Write down five tangible ways the Spirit is calling you to express love and appreciation to your Heavenly Father. Also write down five ways He is calling you to love your neighbor, husband, wife, kids, father, mother, or employer, and yes even your enemy.

PRAYER

Abba Father I pray for the gift of your Holy Spirit to be my guide on this journey to your heart. May he reveal to me the powerful work of your Son Jesus Christ and liberate me from the bondage of sin. May he empower me and equip me with the mind of Jesus Christ so that I can love you with my whole being and live a life of love and forgiveness to my neighbors around me. Father I am aware of my powerlessness and the great need to be directed by your Spirit. Right now I surrender and I ask your Spirit to control my life for your glory, Amen!

❖

JOURNAL/NOTES

CHAPTER 5

THE FAVOR OF FORGIVENESS

The lady who confronted me one Sunday after church about my "striving spirit," was Lynn Brookside. At the time of her piercing words, I wasn't sure I wanted to let Lynn into my life; however, this precious saint became God's marvelous grace to me and a multitude of others. Every Saturday morning, there would be a small group of people that would show up and pray in the sanctuary of our church. Lynn was one of the faithful who never missed. The prayer time was to last an hour, but many times it would go on for three or four hours, and God's Spirit moved in and brought a wellspring of the Father's healing hands.

On one of these Saturdays after a season of prayer, Lynn broke in with these words, "Pastor Tim, may we pray over you? I sense God is calling you to forgive some people in your life." Talk about humbling. I'm the pastor; I should have this forgiveness thing down, right? But the Spirit had been working on my pride, and even though I wasn't sure where Lynn was going with this, I agreed and the prayer group gathered around me, and for the next two hours, I was overcome with emotion as God exposed my heart of unforgivingness.

God had given Lynn a gift to discern some deep-seeded bitterness going way back to early childhood days, likely stemming from my father's alcoholism. Personally I had thought I had broadly covered my dad with forgiveness some years before, but God was showing Lynn a fearful young boy that had stuffed fear and bitterness deep in the back of a closet of his hurt mind where the enemy was still working. Lynn had me forgive every episode from childhood that the Holy Spirit brought to mind. As if my father was there, I said, "Dad I forgive you for _____, " and I would move on to the next event.

After a tear-filled session of offering forgiveness to my father, I felt I had come to the end; exhausted I was ready to drag myself home and take a long nap. But Lynn looked at me and said, "Tim, there is one more person you need to forgive." My flesh was too weak to protest, and I said, "Really?!" I could not think of anyone. "Who?" I asked. She responded, "God!" Now, after getting a degree in Biblical studies in college and taking three years of seminary, I protested. Never had I heard in all my studies that you need to forgive God. I said to Lynn, "God does not sin, how I can forgive Him?"

She responded, "You teach us about the sovereignty of God, a doctrine you say is the foundation to Scripture and all of life, right? But, deep down, you hold God responsible for allowing the deep periods of pain in your life because you believe He is in control of everything that happens, don't you?" She was right. I resisted admitting it, but there was bitterness in my heart toward the Father God for allowing the trials and appearing so distant during those times. Even though it didn't make sense at the time, I said "God I forgive you for allowing these things to happen; I release you." I also prayed that God would forgive me for years of hidden bitterness toward both my earthly and Heavenly Fathers.

That Saturday was a major turning point in healing my father wounds and leading me to understanding the Father's unfailing love for me. That day like no other helped me as a pastor recognize the seriousness of unforgiveness and how it will affect our awareness of the Father's presence in our lives. The Holy Spirit began to reveal Scriptures to me concerning the importance of forgiveness. For the first time, I understood in my heart Jesus' words at the end of the Lord's Prayer: *"For if you forgive men when they sin against you, your heavenly Father will also forgive you. But if you do not forgive men their sins, your Father will not forgive your sin"* (Matthew 6:14-15).

These words of scripture started to unfold and become clearer; if I do not forgive as I have been forgiven by the Father shown at the cross, I will not experience the favor of the Father's face shining on my life. Yes, if I have come to Christ and received the cross, I am forgiven, but if I hold back forgiveness to others, there will be a wall between the Father and me. The relationship I most need in life will be strained by my rebellion, and the secure warmth of His love will feel distant at best. We see this taught elsewhere as well; the disciple John states: *"We love because He first loved us. If anyone says, 'I love God,' yet hates his brother, he is a liar. For anyone who does not love his brother, whom he has seen, cannot love God whom he has not seen"* (1 John 4:19-21).

Paul makes a similar point when he says in Ephesians 4:26-32, "In your anger do not sin. Do not let the sun go down while you are still angry, and do not give the devil a foothold....And do not grieve the Holy Spirit of God, with whom you were sealed for the day of redemption. Get rid of all bitterness, rage and anger, brawling and slander, along with every form of malice. Be kind and compassionate to one another, forgiving each other just as in Christ God forgave you."

When we hang on to bitterness and unforgiveness, we open a wide door for the enemy to come into our lives and build a stronghold from which to work. And he will build fast in order to make a barrier that will keep us from experiencing the presence of the Father's love.

By far forgiveness and the lack of it is the biggest issue I have faced in pastoral counseling. There are so many people today that have strongholds built around their hearts because of an unforgiving spirit. The results are devastating; divorce, addictions, major health problems, lives gripped by fear and insecurity, a striving, controlling spirit, and the absence of joy, peace, and the fullness of the Father's love.

My favorite book on forgiveness is Total Forgiveness by R.T. Kendall; I have handed out hundreds of copies of this book over the years to people imprisoned by unforgiveness. The theme of the book is to bring you to a place of total forgiveness, which means coming to a place where you can pray that God would bless the person who hurt you in the same way that He would bless you. Think of the people that have hurt you in your life. Can you right now pray a blessing over them, asking God to bless them with all the benefits of heaven's love that you desire God to bring to you? If you can't, you know there is work to do. May the Holy Spirit empower you to speak forgiveness right now over those who have wounded you. Stop right now and ask the Holy Spirit to help you do this. You may need help as I did; go to a pastor, a godly friend, a prayer warrior, a counselor, Alcoholics Anonymous (AA) or Narcotics Anonymous (NA) meeting, or buy the book Total Forgiveness; do whatever it takes to work through and daily practice forgiveness.

The price is way too high not to forgive; you don't want anything to stand in the way of encountering Abba Father and an authentic love not of this world. The act of forgiveness is an act of obedience; you may not feel any better at the time of doing it. For me, I felt completely wiped out; I was overcome by an avalanche of emotions. For a season afterward I could not notice a dramatic change in my feelings toward the Father. But in time, I promise you that the feelings will catch up to the act of obedience and the light of the Father's love will meet you in a personal way that speaks directly to your heart. Come into the favor of the Father I promise you it will give you true freedom.

❖

CONTINUE YOUR JOURNEY:

1. Jesus makes this radical statement right after His teaching on the Lord's Prayer; "For if you forgive men when they sin against you, your heavenly Father will also forgive you. But if you do not forgive men their sins, your Father will not forgive your sin (Matthew 6:14-15).

According to these words of Jesus it appears that our forgiveness from the Father is conditional on us forgiving others who have hurt us. How do you understand these verses and the effects of unforgiveness?

I believe the Bible clearly teaches that Christ's death for my sins has forever made me right with God (Romans 3:21-26), however when I withhold forgiveness my relationship with the Father is strained and it is as if His presence has left me. Have you ever experienced a strain in your relationship with the Father because of unforgiveness?

2. Read Paul's potent words to the church of Ephesus on this subject of forgiveness (Ephesians 4:26-32).

An unforgiving spirit will give "the devil a foothold," (vs. 27). Describe what this "foothold" would look like in a person who does not forgive? Have you every allowed this to happen in your heart? If so share the effects of this invasion by the enemy.

Another result of unforgiveness is "grieving the Holy Spirit of God with whom you were sealed for the day of redemption." We know the Holy Spirit is the third person of the Trinity, how do you think He is grieved by lack of forgiveness?

Paul ends vs. 32 with this great challenge "...forgiving each other just as in Christ God forgave you." Think about all the ways you have sinned against your Father in Heaven and how through the blood of Jesus all your sins have been completely washed away. How does this picture of the Father's forgiveness motivate you to forgive another who has hurt you?

3. In this chapter I share how I was challenged to "forgive God."

What do you think about the idea of forgiving God the Father?

Have you ever been bitter at God for allowing painful or harmful things to happen to you?

4. In R.T. Kendall's book Total Forgiveness, he makes the point that true forgiveness is evident when you are able to ask God to bless the person who has hurt you in the same way God would bless you.

Can you pray God's blessing right now over a particular person or people that have hurt you in the past or in the present? If not, God is calling you right now to the obedient act of forgiveness.

JOURNEY DEEPER

Please pick up Total Forgiveness by R.T. Kendall; this is the best book on forgiveness that I have read. He has also published two other great books on this subject, Forgiving Yourself & Forgiving God. Write a letter of forgiveness to the person or people who have hurt you. After you have completed this task, dispose of the letter as a symbol of releasing them. Find a friend, counselor, or pastor who can help you work through the process of forgiveness.

PRAYER

Abba Father I have learned from your Word that forgiveness is vital for a genuine relationship with you. Please give me the strength to forgive _____ for the pain and harm he/she has caused me. Holy Spirit please show me the forgiveness I have received at the cross from the Father through Jesus' sacrifice. Let His powerful blood that has covered me of all my sins empower me to obediently forgive others. Father please forgive me for allowing the enemy to get a foothold in my life through my bitterness toward others and even you dear Father. In Jesus' name I break this stronghold through forgiveness, and I pray a blessing over all who have hurt me. In Jesus' great name, Amen!

❖

JOURNAL/NOTES

CHAPTER 6

OUR HEART'S HOME

It had been a little over three months since my soul searching prayer session with Lynn, and I knew God had done a powerful work in my life. Patty, the two kids and I packed up the car and drove up to Sun Valley, California, where my mom and step-dad lived, to retreat for a few days from the hectic weeks of ministry. Their home was a haven for us during that season of life. Bill, my step- father, had been a pastor for several years, and God in His goodness brought him into our lives about four years earlier as I was just starting out as a pastor. Bill was one of the voices of God's Spirit that would speak wisdom and encouragement, and understood the burden placed on the shoulders of pastors. I hear Bill's voice often in the back of my head saying, "Tim, don't be fearful or worry about all the stuff of ministry; just preach the Word and let God take care of the rest." How right he was; this truth from God has kept me going during some fierce spiritual battles and all out attacks from the enemy.

During our stay those few days, Bill suggested that we go and check out a Christian bookstore nearby that he thought we would like. Little did I know as we entered the store that this was a divine set up. God had this day all planned out; He knew I loved books and He often spoke to me through visuals. With my son in my arms, my heart found its true home; I saw the picture of God the Father holding the young boy wearing the football helmet. Every time I reflect back to that life-altering moment, my heart does a jig inside; a sense of joy invades the veins.

We bought that picture that day and since then bought two more. One hangs in my son's room, one in our bathroom, and one in my office at church. I can't tell you how many times I have pulled it off the shelf and retold the story of that day. The conversation starts like this; "Let me tell you about my Abba Father experience. That boy in the arms of the Father is me. He has always been there even in the darkest moments; He was there with me in the front yard playing football by myself, looking for acceptance and love, a little boy fearful of the world and even the Father. But He was there waiting for me to notice Him waiting for me to realize how much He loved me...."

Three months earlier, the Holy Spirit helped remove some huge walls of bitterness through forgiveness, and for the first time in my life, I knew the Father's love in a deeper, richer way than ever before. I felt fear flee as I was overcome by the face of the Father's glory, shining through Jesus. Any guess what I preached about the next Sunday? You got it, Abba Father, from Romans 8:15. Any time I can share the story I will; either one-on-one or from the pulpit I want everyone to know the healing power of the Father's love.

From that day on, Romans 8:15 has become my passion; it reads; *"For you did not receive a spirit that makes you a slave again to fear, but you received the Spirit of sonship [some versions say "adoption"].* And by him we cry, 'Abba Father.' The work of the Holy Spirit is to bring us to the healing place in our lives from which we can yell out from our hearts that we have a Daddy who makes all the wrongs right (Romans 8:28). We are all born codependent, which means we were created to be dependent on God. But because of sin, we have been left with this awful emptiness that we daily try to fill with the stuff of the world that is never enough. So we become dependent on others, money, religion, addiction, power, pleasure, etc. It is out of the fear of not belonging that these things control us and the only answer to release this striving for this emptiness with what the world offers is Abba!

Notice Paul says, "You did not receive a spirit that makes you a slave again to fear." Through Christ, the walls that separated us from Abba have been broken down; we are not slaves controlled by fear, but faith in the work of Christ opens us up to being sons and daughters of God. I love these next words, "But you received the Spirit [the Holy Spirit] of sonship...."

❖

These are some of the most incredible, loved-filled words to me in the entire bible. As anyone one who has adopted kids knows adoption is costly and an act of sacrificial love.

I have a couple of crazy friends, crazy in the world's eyes anyway. One friend was married with six kids and the other with three. At the same time, God tugged on both families' hearts to adopt a child from Africa. Now, my friends are hard working guys, but financially both of them are far from affluent. The amount of money and energy to adopt children from a foreign country, especially Africa, is overwhelming. But my brothers went for it in faith and found God absolutely faithful. You would have thought one child would be enough after all the money, energy and time it took, but the crazy thing is as I'm writing this, one of my friends just emailed me that they are looking to adopted a third child and possibly the sibling which would make four added to their six; that is crazy love.

When I asked my friend Steve why he would keep adopting, he said they did it because the first time was such an incredible experience with God that they wanted to taste it again. These men would share that adopting kids at a huge cost helped them understand the Heavenly Father's love for them. My other friend, Arnie shared with me that he loves his adopted son just as much as his own children. This experience reminded Arnie of just how much God love him and accepts him as a son. Our Abba God paid a huge price to get us; it cost His pride and joy, a very part of His being, His only Son. When we begin to awaken to the costly love of the Father to bring us home to His heart, transformation begins to happen and fear diminishes in our lives.

The word "adoption" that Paul uses in Romans is powerful. In the Greek, it is made up of two words, huios (son) and thesis (place). Put together it signifies the place and condition of a son given to one to whom it does not naturally belong. When Paul wrote this letter, Roman law required that the adopter be a male and childless; the one to be adopted had to be an independent adult able to agree to be adopted. In the eyes of the law, the adopted one became a new creature; he was regarded as being born again into the new family. Paul picks up on this law and uses this illustration to point out our new status as new creatures in the family of God. The apostle John captures this well when he says, *"Behold what manner of love the Father has bestowed on us that we should be called the sons of God..."* (1 John 3:1).

As sons and daughters through Christ and the work of the Spirit in us, the words "Abba Father" have tremendous meaning. "Abba" is a term used in bible times intended to be a personal name for father; today we would say, "Daddy," or "Papa." In Jewish tradition, a slave could not call his master "Abba;" only sons and daughters had that privileged. Abba is the word framed by the lips of infants, and promises unreasoning trust. The word "Father" expresses a reverent awe of the relationship and realizes that God as our Father is the leader of my life. The two words Abba and Father together express the love and respectful confidence of the child. Can you read these words and cry out "Daddy Father?" This is where Abba desires you to be, to come back home, to rest in His arms and to experience your full rights as sons and daughters.

We look again to Jesus to see how the Abba Father relationship empowered His life. He needed the love of the Father to carry out the mission to bring the lost children home. Remember, He was not only fully God but also fully human. I strongly believe that as he walked the dusty roads of Israel he ministered out of His humanity, and in his humanity, he needed the assurance of the Father's love. Jesus did not start his public ministry until he was anointed at His baptism by the gift of the Holy Spirit, along with the words of the Father, *"You are my Son, whom I love; with you I am well pleased"* (Luke 3:22). As Jesus came out of the waters of the Jordan, the Holy Spirit came down and sealed the Father's love upon His heart. That day there was no doubt in Jesus' mind that he belonged, and He was moved forward in the boldness of that all consuming love.

Do you remember where the Holy Spirit led Jesus right after that mountain top experience of hearing the Father's love? He was led right into a wilderness where he would be in a 40-day spiritual wrestling match with Satan. Why did Jesus overcome the enticing temptations of the serpent? Because nothing that the devil offered--food, fame, or worldly power-could come close to the Father's love.

Jesus overcame the darkness and brought a new kingdom of light into the world fueled by the Holy Spirit and the love of his Abba. He knew that He would have to daily connect with the Father and pray for the Spirit so he would daily seek the Father's face in prayer. We see this in Luke 9, where Jesus climbs up a mountain with three of His disciples and prays. As He is praying, God's glory shows up and announces affirming words in front of the three. *"This is my Son, whom I have chosen, listen to Him"* (vs. 35). We see Jesus' reliance on the Father's love as he was going through the valley of the shadow of death in the Garden of Gethsemane; he cries; *"Abba Father… Everything is possible for you. Take this cup from me. Yet not what I will, but what you will"* (Mark 14:36). He was saying, "Daddy, I need your help!" It was the assurance of his Father's love that sustained him to and on the cross, and it was the Spirit's power and the Father's love that raised Christ from the dead and crowned him King (Romans 8:11).

If Jesus could not do life and ministry without an encounter with his Abba's heart, how can we? Christ knew this and that is why you see in the beginning of the book of Acts Jesus telling His disciples not to leave Jerusalem until they have received "the gift my Father promised you" (1:4). They needed that same love poured over them by the Holy Spirit as Jesus received at His baptism. When the gift came after 10 days of waiting and praying, the disciples, like their Master, were filled up with the love of the Father, which gave them boldness and courage that they had never had before. Peter, who denied Jesus three times the day of His death, now publicly shouted not only that he knew Jesus but also that Jesus was God's Son come to save the world and restore people to the Father; and that day, 3000 came to know the loving heart of the Father.

The early followers of Christ learned to rely on Abba's love and the power of the Holy Spirit as we see in Acts 4; in the midst of a challenge, they stop and seek the face of the Father in prayer, and Abba shows up and fills them up again with the Holy Spirit (vs. 31). The early church's dependence on the Father's love turned a culture upside down as many came into the Father's house.

Jesus reveals to us that the Father's greatest passion for you is to know His massive arms of love reaching out to you. After Jesus teaches His followers the Lord's Prayer in Luke 11, he adds a story about a man who needed bread badly. This man had some friends come over late at night and had nothing to give them; his pantry was empty, not a good host. So he goes over to his neighbors at midnight and bangs loudly on the door. The friends said. "Go away, we are all sleeping." But the desperate man would not relent from his pounding. After some time the neighbor gets up and gives him the bread he needs. Jesus' point is that we need to keep knocking on heaven's door, never giving up until the door opens and Abba pours out His love to feed our hungry souls.

Jesus ends the teaching by saying: *"Which of you fathers, if your son asks for a fish will give him a snake instead? Or if he asks for an egg, will give him a scorpion? If you then, though you are evil know how to give good gifts to your children, how much more will your Father in heaven give the Holy Spirit to those who ask Him"* (vs. 11-13)! My greatest need and your greatest need is the Father's love. Notice the great promise in the words above, "How much more...." The Father wants to send the Holy Spirit upon His children and fill them with heaven's love. Keep knocking on heaven's door until it opens and you find your heart's true home.

CONTINUE YOUR JOURNEY:

1. As I shared in the introduction to the book and in this chapter my life was forever changed as I looked at the picture of the little boy wearing the football helmet in the arms of the Heavenly Father. I call it my "Abba, Father experience." Read carefully and slowly Romans 8:12-17.

In the beginning of verse 15 Paul says; "For you did not receive a spirit that makes you a slave again to fear..." Describe how fear in your life has kept you in slavery?

But according to Paul in verse 15b what breaks the stronghold of "fear" in our lives?

One of the greatest works of the Holy Spirit is the revelation of our "adoption" or "sonship" as some translations use. How does it make you feel that you have been brought into this family through the work of your brother Jesus?

The Spirit ignites our spirits to "cry out, 'Abba, Father." Why does the Spirit move our hearts to use these two terms for God?

If you know God as your "Abba" (Daddy) who is also your "Father" whom you deeply respect as the leader of your life, what belongs to you according to verses 16,17?

2. The "Abba, Father" relationship was what empowered the life and mission of Jesus; read Luke 3:21-22 and Luke 9:28-36.

I believe that Jesus is both fully God and man, but during his time on earth I believe that Jesus did ministry in his humanity. Do you agree or disagree? How does your response relate to the power that resides within each of us as believers?

Why do you think it is significant that the Holy Spirit showed up at Jesus' baptism and He heard the Father say; "You are my Son, whom I love; with you I am well pleased?"

In Luke 4 we see Jesus "full of the Holy Spirit" being lead into the wilderness to battle Satan for 40 days. What enabled Jesus defeat the lies and temptations of the enemy?

In the story of the "transfiguration of Jesus"(Luke 9:28-36) we see Jesus climbs the mountain with three of his disciples to pray to His Father, for he knows his death on the cross is coming soon. What are the ways that the Father encourages His Son in this mission?

3. As I state in the book, "If Jesus could not do life and ministry without an encounter with his "Abba's heart, how can we?"

According to Acts 1:4-8 what did the disciples need and what do we need before we seek to follow in the footsteps of Jesus?

*After the outpouring of the Holy Spirit in Acts 2 we see a church empowered by the love of the Father to do courageous things. **Read Acts 4:23-31**. How did the early church remain in that powerful love relationship with the Father?*

What do you think is the greatest need for the church today in our present cultural crisis?

JOURNEY DEEPER

Read and mediate on Jesus' teaching found in Luke 11:1-13. Continue to wait and pray for the "gift of the Father," until He comes and reveals to you the empowering love of "Abba, Father." Remember God will meet you where you are at; He will use His Word, prayer, praise, pictures, people and places to show you His unquenchable love. Continue to keep "asking", "seeking," and "knocking."

Write a letter with your name on it from your "Abba, Father." Remember as the Father affirmed Jesus and spoke words of love over him at his baptism and transfiguration, he does the same over you and all who are in Christ.

PRAYER

Abba Father, my greatest need in life is to experience your love for me. A love that testifies to my spirit that I am your very own son or daughter. That you gave up your only Son Jesus Christ to bring me home and to show me your true feelings for me. Abba I pray for the gift of your Holy Spirit to open my spiritual ears to hear, "you are my son/daughter whom I love; with you I am well pleased," Amen!

✣

JOURNAL/NOTES

CHAPTER 7

SONS AND DAUGHTERS OF THE _____

One of the blessings of modern technology is that you can communicate visually with someone on the other side of the world. My oldest daughter, Sarah, is in South Africa as I am writing, and last night we talked face-to-face amazing! She was just getting up and I was getting ready for bed. It was a blessing catching up and seeing her beautiful face and as we said our goodbyes I ended with, "Daughter of the _____!" And she promptly responded, "King!"

That interchange goes all the way back to when she started her first day of school. On that very first day of leaving mom and dad and entering a world where she would spend a good portion of the day away from us, I wanted her to know to whom she belonged. Her Dad was the King of the Universe, and even though her earthly parents could not be physically present with her, her Abba, the King, watched over her every minute of the day. So almost every morning since Sarah's first day of school, my three kids have heard this statement and filled in the blank with King!

It is so important in a world filled with insecurity and fear to be reminded that you belong; you are loved by the Father, Son, and Holy Spirit. There is a great historic confession, written 500 years ago, that summarizes this belonging best:

Q: What is your only comfort in life and in death?

A: That I am not my own but belong body and soul in life and in death to my faithful Savior Jesus Christ. He has fully paid for all my sins with his precious blood, and has set me free from the tyranny of the devil. He also watches over me in such a way that

not a hair can fall from my head without the will of my Father in
heaven: in fact, all things must work together for my salvation.
Because I belong to him, Christ by his Holy Spirit assures me of
eternal life and make me whole-heartedly willing and ready from
now on to live for him (Heidelberg Catechism, Lord's Day 1).

Every day we need to confess this belonging. In fact, for centuries parents and churches had children memorize that statement above, knowing that if you live into these truths, you will experience a life of spiritual victories.

For Paul, to know Abba's love was foundational; the heart of Romans 8 is verse 15, which speaks of that glorious adoption given to us when we know our belonging, and cry "Abba Father." But if you keep reading Romans 8, you see the result of this is "The Spirit himself testifies with our spirit that we are God's children. Now if we are children, then we are heirs – heirs of God and co-heirs with Christ, if indeed we share in his sufferings in order that we may also share in his glory."

Did you catch that? You not only have a Father who loves you as His very own, but you also have a Father who gives you all that is His; everything that He has given to Christ we share in. Through the suffering of the cross, by dying daily to self, we are resurrected with Christ into a glorious inheritance that is not just coming in the future; it starts the moment you trust in the gift of salvation that the Father has given you.

Where is Christ right now? The bible teaches that 40 days after His resurrection he took his seat on the throne the Father has given Him. Jesus is King right now; this very moment He is reigning over the world. For the last several years there has been a popular theology that emphasizes Christ's reign coming in the future, and many have spent too much time thinking about when that is going to happen and what will it look like, and miss the fact He reigns now. Don't miss the biblical teaching of Christ's Lordship over everything this very moment because the implications are huge for His children.

Paul prays this incredible prayer for believers found in the book of Ephesians 1:18-21

I pray also that the eyes of your heart may be enlightened in order that you may know the hope to which he has called you, the riches of his glorious inheritance in the saints, and his incomparably great power for us who believe. That power is like the working of his mighty strength, which he exerted in Christ when he raised him from the dead and seated him at his right hand in the heavenly realms, far above all rule and authority, power and dominion.

In this scripture Paul demonstrates that fact that Christ is the ruling at this very moment. We as God's children are heirs with Christ; we have been given the same power; from the Greek we get our word dynamite, this power is what raised Christ from the dead and this power lives in us. Paul goes on to say that this "power" places Christ as the universal King right now. It gets even better; Paul goes on to say, "And God raised us up with Christ and seated us with him in the heavenly realms in Christ Jesus" (Ephesians 2:6). This declaration states that currently you are royalty, you share now in the rule of Christ, and the enemy is under your feet as spiritually you have the best seat in the house. All that belongs to your older brother Jesus you share with him at this very moment.

Don't you see why the enemy wants to keep you from knowing the love of Abba Father? Why he will do all in his power to blind our eyes from seeing the true reality of our position through Christ? If we start to realize Abba's love and the "glorious riches" now given to us along with our reign with Christ now, the Kingdom of God will flood out of us like a rushing river bringing glory to our Father. My Dad is King of the universe, reigning through His Son; and as His adopted son, I'm a part of it all. Oh, what a mind blowing thought. The more that I understand the better I will live into my glorious calling as a beloved son.

Our first parents Adam and Eve were called to rule in the garden and expand that rule to the rest of the earth. The key to their rule was their relationship with their Father. Remember who was also living on earth at that time? The answer is Satan, who was cast out of heaven along with a group of fallen angels (Revelation 12:7-9). As long as Adam and Eve stayed in that love relationship with the Father, they would expand His glory all over the earth. The enemy knew this as well; he saw the threat and he knew he needed to get them to stop trusting in the Father's love, to live apart from His presence. As a result, our first parents lost that personal fellowship with the Father, lost identity, and lost their Kingdom purpose to bring the Father's reign on earth.

But the Father's plan to restore that broken relationship, identity, and reign was promised in Genesis 3:15, where a promised Savior would come from the seed of the woman and would crush the head of the dragon and bring God's Kingdom back to earth. This reign broke into the world in the life, death, resurrection, and reign of Christ Jesus. Now, as He brings us back to relationship with the Father, we are empowered with the Spirit of the King to overcome the darkness with the great news, that in Christ, we have been made sons and daughters of the King who go forth bringing His love and glory to the world.

That is why it is so important every day that you are reminded that you are sons and daughters of the King! The world and all the enemies of God will do everything they can to keep you from living into that reality. One of the greatest tools the enemy uses to do that today is to keep you busy, filling your life with activities, some even good, that you miss the voice of your Father. We work more, eat more, play more, indulge more, spend more, study more, strive more; we even try to serve more than ever before but have lost more of the awareness of Abba's love and our glorious inheritance that comes with it.

A few years ago, I sensed that I was losing the still small voice of God's love and was getting caught up in the endless cycle of busyness. So I took a day off from the endless demands of ministry and life with three teenagers, and got into my car and hurried down to spend time with the Lord at the beach. I got on Hwy 91, the worst freeway in the United States and, true to its name, was trapped in the wilderness of angry drivers as traffic came to a complete stop. I joined in their bitterness as I had a wonderful day planned being with God in the beauty of His creation. In the seat next to me was God, or at least His voice in the form of my bible. I kept feeling the nudge to pick it up as I fumed in traffic. Earlier that morning before I left, I was reading Psalm 46, so I opened it up to that song and read it again hoping that would open up the bottleneck. No such luck. Instead, I was prompted to start to memorize it, thinking I needed to make the most of this wasted time. As I worked though the verses, the Spirit shouted to my spirit these words: "Be still and know that I am God" (vs. 10). When I finally made it to the ocean, all I could hear above the breaking waves was "Be still…" I knew God was calling me back to slow down and take the time needed to listen for the Father's voice of love and affirmation. I too slipped into the fast lane of busyness and struggled to hear the most important voice of all.

As a result of that day, I made it my goal to learn to become "still" again and remember that my Dad is King and I'm His son. Here are some things that helped me in my journey towards stillness over the last few years:

1. **Scripture.** Read it slowly and meditatively. My personality pushes me to accomplish, and I can do that in my bible reading as well. At times I would rush through my devotional reading to conquer as many chapters as I could that day instead of letting God use one word or one verse to speak to my heart.

2. **Silence.** Instead of doing all the talking during my prayer time I try to still my mind, so hard to do, and sit and listen to the promptings of the Spirit. To let what I just read in the Word be God's voice to me. I let God talk also through meditating on the beauty of His creation. To sit and gaze at the mountains, trees, ocean, wildlife, or listen to a river rumble down the mountain, and realize that my Abba made it all.

3. **Seek his face.** I have found that worship is one of the greatest ways to encounter the presence of Abba's grace. I can't sing a lick so I will listen to others who can and join them seeking after the face of God. I can't dance either, but when I'm all alone and sing and dance before the Lord, I sense His pleasure.

4. **Slow down.** Another word for this is "fasting." Fasting for a season from food, Starbucks (ouch) and the media have allowed me to renew, reconnect, and be refilled by the rhythm of His heart.

5. **Service.** The more I get out of myself and serve others, especially those who can't always give back, the more I encounter God's face. I have seen Jesus so real in prisoners, orphans in Africa, the homeless, the sick, and in those with special needs.

6. Sabbath rest. The Father created our DNA to experience His affections powerfully by spending one day a week resting in His presence. I normally take Friday's off but that day is filled up with work around the house and catching up on other things. So in the last year I have tried to set Monday's aside to enjoy His presence through prayer, reading, and enjoying His creation.

7. Sabbatical. This can be a weekend or a week retreat focused on growing in the knowledge of God's love. My church has given me the rich blessing of a three month sabbatical that I'm presently on in order to pause and regain the awareness of the Father's favor. After 22 years of full time ministry, I have been able to step back for a moment from the role of a pastor to just be a son.

This season of "stillness" and practicing these seven spiritual disciplines has driven me back to the "love that surpasses knowledge." I pray that you will join me in "being still" in a busy world so we together can claim, "We are sons and daughter of the _____!" And by knowing this truth, we will explode into our communities with His Kingdom power and show a longing world what the Father's love looks like.

I leave you with one of the greatest prayers in all of Scripture that your Father wants to desperately grant to you this day:"I pray that out of his glorious riches he may strengthen you with power through the Spirit in your inner being, so that Christ may dwell in your hearts through faith. And I pray that you, being rooted and established in love, may have power, together with all the saints, to grasp how wide and long and high and deep is the love of Christ, and to know this love that surpasses knowledge – that you may be filled to the measure of all the fullness of God. Now to him who is able to do immeasurably more than all we ask or imagine, according to his power that is at work within us, to him be glory in the church and in Christ Jesus throughout all generations, forever and ever! Amen" (Ephesians 3:16-21).

✤

CONTINUE YOUR JOURNEY:

1. The historic confession, the Heidelberg Catechism, starts out by asking the question "What is your only comfort in life and in death?" Truly, this is one of the greatest questions you will every ask yourself.

So how would you answer this question?

As you recall from reading this chapter the answer is all about "belonging" to God the Father, Son and Holy Spirit. Describe your thoughts on what it looks like to belong to this incredible God?

One of the greatest and most overlooked events in biblical history is the ascension of Christ to the throne of heaven forty days after His resurrection. Why is this event so important to the understanding of "belonging" according to Ephesians 1:18-21?

❖

Paul makes this mind-blowing declaration in Ephesians 2:6; "And God raised us up with Christ and seated us with him in the heavenly realms in Christ Jesus." Stop, pause, and reread that again slowly. According to these words where are you seated right now and how should that verse impact your life?

Why is it important that every day you are reminded that you are sons and daughters of the King? And how does the enemy try to distract you from this truth?

✧

2. Take a moment and prayerfully read Psalm 46. The author of this Psalm opens up with the words *"God is our refuge and strength an ever-present help in times of trouble. Therefore we will not fear...."*

Here is a declaration of true belonging and a true knowledge of God as your Father. I believe vs. 10 holds the key to being able to live out this statement, "be still and know that I am God." Describe what being "still" means?

In this chapter I list seven things that have helped me journey towards "stillness" (Scripture, Silence, Seek his face, Slow down, Service, Sabbath rest, & Sabbatical). Choose a couple of these as described in the book and share how they have helped you hear the Father's voice in a noisy world?

From the list describe the one that is hardest for you to practice and why?

Make a commitment with each other to learn to "be still" by putting one or more of these seven disciplines into practice.

JOURNEY DEEPER

Seek to daily find a spiritual rhythm that will help you hear the voice of your Father so that you can live into the fullness as a son or daughter of the King. Read Richard J. Foster's Celebration of Discipline. This is one of the best books on spiritual disciplines that will help you grow in your understanding and in the practice of hearing Abba's voice.

PRAYER

Pray Paul's prayer from Ephesians 3:16-21:

I pray that out of his glorious riches he may strengthen you with power through the Spirit in your inner being, so that Christ may dwell in your hearts through faith. And I pray that you, being rooted and established in love, may have power, together with all the saints, to grasp how wide and long and high and deep is the love of Christ, and to know this love that surpasses knowledge – that you many be filled to the measure of all the fullness of God. Now to him who is able to do immeasurable more than all we ask or imagine, according to his power that is at work within us, to him be glory in the church and in Christ Jesus throughout all generations, forever and ever! Amen

❖

JOURNAL/NOTES

CHAPTER 8

BLESSING THE FATHER

Recently I was back in the Rocky Mountains for a few weeks to visit family and spend some time at a silent retreat center outside of Denver. As I was walking around the beautiful grounds of the retreat center and catching glances of the snow-covered Rockies, my thoughts reflected to a few days earlier where I spent the day working with my dad. It had been years since I had been in a cement truck and experienced the rumble of a powerful diesel engine. My dad was short of help that day, so he had to deliver a load of concrete and I rode along.

I have to tell you that it was sort of fun pretending for a day that I was in the cement business and not a pastor. As we were unloading the truck, my dad could tell that the young men struggled to keep up with the pour, so he grabbed a shovel and started to help. I jumped in the truck and moved it back and forth into the right position, directed by my dad running the controls in the back. As we drove away, there was a sense of accomplishment as we could see a successfully finished product, and I also felt the joy of working side by side with my father.

As I walked the dirt path of the retreat center warmed by the Colorado sun, I realized I felt pride for my father that day. My dad, in his seventies, still worked hard and graciously helped some young contractors finish a job that was too big for their inexperience. As I pondered that moment, I sensed a deep need to tell my dad my feelings, to let him know how proud I was of his hard work, his graciousness and how he over the years demonstrated a spirit of perseverance.

That night in the quietness of the retreat center as I wrote these thoughts in my journal, I had one of those quickening times by the Spirit that enlightened me to my Heavenly Father's heart. It was as if God was saying to me, "That feeling of pride that you have for your dad and desire to tell him is the same attitude I long for from my children." Our Abba wants us to be proud of Him and His mighty work in creation and in the recreation of our lives through Christ. We have been created to boast in our Daddy, to tell the world of His amazing works of love for His children.

The journey to the Father's heart will always bring us to this place, to a deep pride and love that needs to be expressed in worship to Him and witnessed to others. The psalmist makes this clear when he says; *"In God we make our boast all day long, and we will praise your name forever"* (Psalm 44:8). As we listen to Jesus' prayer the night before the cross we notice this was His greatest passion: *"Father, the time has come. Glorify your Son, that your Son may glorify you. For you granted him authority over all people that he might give eternal life to all those you have given him. Now this is eternal life: that they know you, the only true God, and Jesus Christ, whom you have sent. I have brought you glory on earth by completing the work you gave me to do. And now, Father, glorify me in your presence with the glory I had with you before the world began"* (John 17:1-4).

As Jesus' passion was for the Father's glory to be known in word and works, so this is where the healing of Abba Father leads us; this is the goal of the journey. The historic Westminster Shorter Catechism proclaims this truth in its first question and answer: "What is the chief end of man?" The answer states: "A man's chief end is to glorify God and to enjoy him forever." When we boast in our Father, when we feel a deep pride for what He has done for us and we tell Him and others, we experience the life for which we were created.

As a pastor, I have experienced thousands of worship experiences over the years. But I would have to say the most moving, life-transforming encounters have been in unlikely places. I will never forget one of my first worship times in the chapel of Corcoran state prison in Central California. In a small room filled with men wearing blue jeans and blue button-up shirts, was an inmate up front who played an out-of-tune guitar with sheet music in front of him. There was no sound system, no Power Point to follow, but once he started the first verse of "Amazing Grace," heaven came down and

God's glory filled the room. I had never heard singing like that before; it came from the depths of souls who had experienced God's deep, unconditional love. Hands were raised up, shouts rolled off lips, eyes closed as men sang, "Amazing grace! How sweet the sound, that saved a wretch like me! I once was lost, but now am found. Was blind but now I see." They held nothing back in the praise and worship to their Savior.

I could not keep this gift of what I witnessed in the prison to myself, and I invited whomever I could to join me in hearing these authentic worship encounters. Once I brought a worship group from a local church in to help lead the worship time. The man who ran the sound that day was named Brian. Brian had grown up going to church twice a Sunday his entire life. But, that day as Brian watched worship from the back of the chapel, he broke as the Holy Spirit overwhelmed him through the worship of the inmates. For the first time in his life, Brian raised both hands in the air and tasted the grace of the Father. After that day, Brian's life would never be the same as he set out on his own journey to the Father's heart.

My other favorite place of worship has been in a little country called Lesotho, Africa, a place that has been devastated by poverty and HIV Aids. I have had the privilege to be in this wonderful place on several occasions, visiting a care center for abandoned babies called Beautiful Gate, founded by good friends, Ray and Sue Haakenson. In the midst of much hardship and brokenness, there is a joy of another world that shows up in worship times that can go on for several hours. Just like the prisons, there are no flashing lights, few instruments, and sound systems that only work sometimes. But those things become meaningless as the singing begins and dancing follows; faces are illuminated with God's glory shining like the noonday sun. The hours seem like minutes as time stands still when God is praised from a heart full of thanksgiving.

These two places have taught me that worship comes from hearts proud of their big God, a God bigger than prison cells, a God more powerful than deadly disease and the limits of poverty. Many in these places have found an Abba Father who has freed them, forgiven them, and opened their eyes to their true identity as sons and daughters of the King. They can testify with the Apostle Paul as he ends glorious chapter 8 of Romans with these words: "Who shall separate us from the love of Christ? Shall trouble or hardship or persecution or famine or nakedness or danger or sword? No, in all these things we are more than conquerors through him who loved us. For I am convinced that neither death nor life, neither angels nor demons, neither the present nor the future, nor any powers, neither height nor depth, nor anything else in all creation, will be able to separate us from the love of God that is in Christ Jesus our Lord" (vs. 35-39).

This is what your Father is looking for; He is looking for you to bless Him, to worship Him. Jesus teaches, "Yet a time is coming and has now come when the true worshipers will worship the Father in spirit and truth, for they are the kind of worshipers the Father seeks" (John 4:23). I translate these words to mean that in Christ, the "truth," we are brought before the Father in the spiritual realm, to encounter His lasting love and respond with unending praise and worship. As we worship and boast all day in His love for us, the blessings of His presence rain down on His children, bringing abundant life.

Desperate for some human conversation after my silent retreat, I drove over to my sister's house and shared some of the insights Abba was revealing to me about blessing both our earthly father and Abba Father. A few days later, my courageous sister Cindy invited my brother's family, my dad and his wife, and me to join her family for Sunday dinner. After our meal, Cindy gathered us together and said, "For devotions today we are going to each go around the room and say a blessing over Dad." So both the grandkids and adults each shared a good memory about Dad and how he has blessed our lives. As we started around the room, the tears quickly came first over my dad and then over most of the 12 of us in the room. Something holy and healing was taking place as words of affirmation were shared.

As the last person finished the time of blessing, my dad responded through his sobs with gratitude and blessings back over us, which filled the room with pools of peace overflowing with waterfalls of love. None of us there will forget that day and the abundant fruit that followed. Again, as I traveled back on the plane to California looking out the window from 33,000 feet marveling at the mountains my Abba had made, I thought of that Sunday time of blessing. The Spirit again pointed out to me, "When you bless me as you blessed your earthly father, I will open the windows of heaven and shower you with my perfect peace."

Lately, the Father has been teaching me to praise and thank Him even when I can't understand what He is doing. The Apostle Paul knows the importance of this in his relationship to the Father, so he commands us to *"Be joyful always; pray continually; give thanks in all circumstance, for this is God's will for you in Christ Jesus"* (1 Thessalonians 5:16-18).

When we can do this in the storms and disappointments in life, we are demonstrating a trust in the Father that will place us high upon a Rock that remains secure against a ragging storm.

Just recently I had a chance to practice this as we got a call from my son TJ who was in the hospital 1600 miles away with a shattered clavicle. He was playing in his very first college football game where he was tackled by some strong farm boys who drove his right shoulder into the astro turf which caused three breaks in his collarbone. They wanted to do surgery the next day, so Patty went to work and got me out on the first flight in the morning. As I sat in the waiting room, I tried to practice 1 Thess. 5:16-17, which is not easy when your child is under the knife and you feel helpless to heal both broken bones and a broken heart. But I tried to give thanks even though it seemed like a bad dream.

For the next few days as I watched my son recover in the motel room far from home, we had trouble finding words, forced some prayers out, read some scriptures over him, and continued to try to give thanks. On Friday I took him back to his dorm room with a painful ache in my heart knowing I would have to leave him there to head back to California early in the morning. Again, words were hard to come by as he lay in his bed and I sat looking out the window at the football field where the injury took place. In our hearts both wondering why, when he finally broke and the tears flowed, we wrestled with why did this happen and what did the future look like as it seemed a dream had been lost. It was a priceless moment we will both never forget as we brought raw hearts to God, after a time of prayer, peace came and I was able to say good bye.

The next morning I continued to give thanks as I sat in the Denver airport writing in my journal about what happened in the dorm room the night before, I received this text from my son, "Slept good until about 4:30 am and then I could not get back to sleep for a while. I read "Jesus Calling" [devotional] this morning so that was good! Yah, some reason I'm here and don't need to fear cause God is with me and was thinking if my earthly father is willing to fly 1600 miles to get here in 24 hrs and how much that meant, how much more does my Heavenly Father love and care for me!!"

Oh, what a gift from the Father to hear my son declare in the midst of pain that he need not fear because the Father's love showed up and he would be taken care of. I could not ask for a more precious gift than that truth given to my only son. Joy filled my soul right in the middle of the airport; how great is my Abba Father, so worthy of praise and thanksgiving. Maybe you are in the midst of a disappointment or a painful situation right now; try thanking your Father, and watch how He will show Himself in the midst of the storm and destroy the fear and replace it with peace.

As we end this journey together to the Father's heart, I want to leave with you a prayer that I pray often. It is the last verse of Jesus prayer in John 17:26, the last request Jesus brings to the Father: "I have made you known to them, and will continue to make you known in order that the love you have for me may be in them, and that I myself may be in them." Jesus prays that you and I would know the same love Jesus feels from the Father; "Jesus knows that there is nothing greater in the entire world than knowing the Father's love. Jesus could endure the worst death in history because He knew the greatest love of eternity. This is what your Father wants the most for you, to know His love. As you put this book down, please take up the prayer of John 17:26, and make ready your heart for an encounter with Abba's soul desire for you- to know His love in such a way that you can cry out, "Abba Father!"

CONTINUE YOUR JOURNEY:

1. Describe a time in your life when you were proud of your earthly father or someone who was a father figure to you. *How did you respond to this feeling of love and pride in your heart?*

2. The journey to the Father's heart will lead you to a place of deep pride and love for your Heavenly Father. Read John 17:1-4 and notice Jesus' passion for the Father.

According to vs. 1 what is the goal behind Jesus' prayer to be "glorified" by the Father?

How does Jesus define "eternal life," in verse 3?

In verse 3 the word for "know" is a deep intimate relationship, much more than head knowledge. Because of Jesus' intimate relationship with the Father what do you think Jesus wants the world to know about his Father?

Read verse 25, the final words of this passionate prayer of Jesus. What is his greatest longing for you to experience that will forever transform your life as it did His?

3. As we have learned from Jesus, our greatest goal in life is to bring glory to our Father through our worship and witness.

Has there been a time when you sensed an overwhelming love and pride in your Heavenly Father? If so, what was your response?

Read Psalm 8, *David's first Hymn of Praise recorded in the Psalms. What causes David to say at the beginning and end of the Psalm, "O LORD, our Lord how majestic is your name in all the earth!"?*

As you take a moment and meditate on your "Abba, Father" and all he has done for you, what words would you use to describe Him?

Now imagine that your "Abba" is sitting in the room with you and speak a blessing of praise.

*In **1 Thessalonians 5:16-18** Paul commands us to "Be joyful always; pray continually and give thanks in all circumstances for this is God's will for you in Christ Jesus." Sometimes the most difficult time to bless your Father is during seasons of heartache and pain when life doesn't make sense. If you are facing a trying time right now, take a moment and lay the problem in your Father's hands and thank him for how he will use it for your good **(Romans 8:28).***

Picture I "found" in the store while holding my 2 year old son!

JOURNEY DEEPER

1) Write a letter of blessing to your earthly father even if he has passed away or you have a strained relationship, and watch how peace will follow.

2) Read a Psalm a day to help open your heart to a spirit of prayer and praise.

3) Spend one hour just listening to praise worship.

4) Read **Ann VosKamp's** *One Thousand Gifts*, a marvelous book that will open you up to the Father's heart through a spirit of thanksgiving.

5) Watch *Ragamuffin*, a film based on the life of Christian song writer Rich Mullins, it is a valuable tool that displays a powerful picture of how words can weigh one down and blessings can release true freedom in Christ.

PRAYER

Make this prayer that comes from Jesus'
prayer in John 17:26 a priority in your life:

Abba Father, I want to know the same powerful love that you have for your Son Jesus in my heart. Abba I know there is no greater love than your perfect love that you have revealed to me through your Son's death. Right now I receive your love by faith and declare with all my heart, "Abba, I belong to you!" Please let me bring glory to your name by how I live pointing the world around me to my Father in Heaven, Amen.

JOURNAL/NOTES

JOURNAL/NOTES

Made in the USA
Middletown, DE
11 February 2021